# ROCK

KATE HODGES

# PAPER

# SCISSORS

✂

SIMPLE, THRIFTY, FUN ACTIVITIES TO KEEP
YOUR FAMILY ENTERTAINED ALL YEAR ROUND

**Photography by Penny Wincer**

*Hardie Grant*

QUADRILLE

CONTENTS

This book is dedicated
to every kid fighting
invisible demons and all
the Type 1 diabetes crew.

# Hello there

**Conjuring up a game, a craft or a story from almost nothing feels like a superpower. But it's a superpower that's easily learned. Rolling a newspaper, giving it a few snips with a pair of scissors and producing a ladder that reaches into the sky. Taking three rocks and starting a laughter-filled, absorbing game of football. Using a simple rock pendant to find water or to discover what the future has in store. What's in this book may be simple – we'll use three core elements of rocks, paper and scissors – but the results are near-magical.**

Do you know how to play the game this book is named after? You'll need two players, but no equipment. It's all about making signs with your hands. A fist is a 'rock', a flat hand 'paper' and your forefinger and index finger make up the 'scissors' sign. Turns are short and sweet. Each player makes one of the signs at exactly the same time. Each sign beats another: rock 'blunts' scissors, scissors 'cut' paper, and paper 'wraps' rock. The winner of each turn is the one who makes the sign that vanquishes the other. It's a good way to decide who gets to go first.

I've always had an interest in unusual rocks and pebbles; as a child I collected exotic crystals and fossils, and that interest has never left me. I still habitually cast my eyes downwards on a beach, picking up sea glass, oddly coloured rocks and, sadly more often, bits of plastic to put in a bin. My kids are equally cursed; during the summer, when we visit the beach most days, my son will offer me my 'daily rock', to be admired and appreciated and then returned to its original spot.

I'm a magpie when it comes to paper, too. I hoard pretty packaging, pick up old magazines and comics at boot fairs, and save Christmas cards and cereal packets with frugal glee. Lots of these projects make use of that hoarding instinct. Yes, you could buy gorgeous craft paper or perfectly flat pebbles, but it's cheaper and more fun to repurpose an old copy of a children's comic into a paper boat.

I've tried to make the projects as universal as possible and have given options for those lucky enough to live near a beach or big park, but the ideas also work for those with a smaller balcony or no outside space. Also, when I refer to 'family' in the book, I don't have a two-parents-two-kids deal in my head, although that is super cool. It's a blanket term which can cover any setup, from a select twosome to a big gathering of friends.

I hope you enjoy trying out the silly, strange and beautiful ideas in this book. Lots of them came from the heads of the silly, strange and beautiful Loulou Cousin (@cousin.loulou) and Jeff Pitcher (@pitcher_post), so go and give them a big round of applause. And I'd love to know what you think of the book and am itching to see your creations and fun; look me up online (@theekatehodges) and drop me a message and pictures.

# Stuff You Will Need

You can complete many of the projects in the book using just rocks, paper and scissors, but it will help enormously if you have a capsule collection of craft kit (try saying that with a cookie in your mouth). None of this is expensive, but if you always have it to hand, you can make pretty much anything on these pages. Some of it will be in your kitchen cupboards, but store the rest in a box that can be taken out at a moment's notice and a whole world will unfold.

★ Felt-tip pens
★ Pencils
★ PVA glue and spreaders
★ Acrylic paints and acrylic paint pens (paint pens aren't super cheap, but they are so brilliant for colouring rocks in bright detail that it's worth investing in a set)
★ Brushes and pots
★ Flour
★ Card (keep old boxes folded flat)
★ Sticky tape or glue dots
★ Ruler

If you'd like to get a little more fancy, here are some more bits you might consider having in your stash.

★ Art paper and card
★ Long rolls of brown or white paper
★ Permanent marker pens
★ Wax crayons
★ Pipe cleaners
★ Clay (buy online or find a squidgy natural source of it near you – try riverbanks or claggy coasts)
★ Stapler
★ Fimo (polymer clay) or Plasticine
★ Googly eyes
★ Hot glue gun or strong glue
★ Craft knife and cutting board
★ Guillotine
★ Stone polisher

**MAGPIE BOX**

As mentioned, I'm a hoarder. Other people might throw away pretty packaging, ribbons and feathers, but I pick them up and keep them for exactly the right time. There will always be a use for something that sparkles. You might like to keep a box of:

★ Tissue paper packaging
★ Newspapers
★ Magazines
★ Greetings cards
★ Tickets
★ Bird feathers
★ Acorn cups
★ Art paper
★ Sweet and candy wrappers
★ Driftwood
★ Music manuscripts
★ Old playing cards
★ Tiny twigs
★ Torn and damaged books

From all these things comes crafty magic. My friend Loulou, who made some of the most beautiful projects in the book, finds old photographs, pictures that make her laugh and pretty patterns and makes colour photocopies of them. If you find anything too precious to use, perhaps you might do the same.

# Key

**Each project in this book is marked with a symbol to show what combination of rocks, paper and scissors you'll need.**

ROCK       PAPER       SCISSORS

# Boring Rules

**There are lots of snoozeworthy safety rules that we need to get straight right from the start and some ethical considerations for the environment around us. Let's put them all here so we can get them out of the way and move on to the good part. Do read them, they're important.**

**1** Most of these projects are fun for older kids to try alone, but some may need adult guidance. Young children will always need supervision, particularly when there are small stones or sharp scissors around.

**2** Small children have a tendency to want to swallow stones, so keep small mouths well away from smaller rocks.

**3** Never take lots of stones from a beach. Just one small pebble or rock might seem fine, but pocketing them destroys habitats and causes the shoreline to erode. Taking stones is even illegal on some beaches, so it's best to admire the prettiest stones and rocks where they are. Never pull stones down from cliffs – it's selfish and dangerous.

**4** If you must, must have a pebble, consider offsetting; for every stone you put in your pocket, take and recycle five pieces of plastic or rubbish. If you're really keen to collect stones, buy them online from ethical, reputable stores.

**5** Don't mess with natural habitats. Leave big stones in rock pools and rivers. They're often home to lots of creatures.

**6** If you make art outside, take a picture, then put everything back where you found it. There's more about this in individual projects, but don't mess with Mother Nature.

**7** Certain stones have a use. Don't touch any that have a purpose, for example way markers or cairns. Some stones are sacred; don't jump or climb on anything that might be meaningful to someone else. Have respect for others' beliefs.

**8** Always use non-toxic paints if you're going to put stone artworks back outside.

**9** Give age-appropriate scissors. Round-ended, safety designs are best until your kids figure out how to keep their fingers away from sharp blades.

**10** Be careful with hot rocks and glue guns. No-one wants a trip to hospital with burned fingers.

**11** Never put water-logged rocks or sedimentary (layered) stones into an oven. They have a tendency to explode.

**12** Always wear safety goggles and long sleeves if you're bashing rocks and don't make sparks near dry grass.

**13** Recycle what you can – paper offcuts, tired projects, as much plastic as you can. Let's show the planet some kindness.

Got all that? Now let's get on with the fun stuff...

# GET CREATIVE

**Rocks, paper and scissors may be basic elements, but combine them cleverly, add a little imagination and you can make pretty much anything.**

# Make and Dye Your Own Paper

**Using old scraps of paper, card and packaging to make a new sheet of paper is not just satisfying and fun, it also teaches us how recycling works. This is a fairly lengthy project, which will keep bubbling along for a few days.**

## YOU'LL NEED

★ Scraps of waste paper, card, newspaper or egg cartons
★ Bucket
★ Potato masher
★ Towel
★ 1 or 2 sheets of parchment paper
★ 2 dish towels
★ Rolling pin

Home-made paper tends to be either grey or the colours of whatever scraps you are using. Try jazzing it up by adding food colouring, flower petals or leaves.

**1** Tear your paper and card into tiny pieces, about 5 x 5cm (2 x 2in) and place in the bucket.

**2** Cover the paper with water and let it soak for a few hours, overnight if possible. If you want to make coloured paper, add a few drops of food colouring to the soaking water (a handful of blackberries foraged from hedgerows also works well).

**3** Keep shredding and tearing the paper into smaller and smaller pieces, and use a potato masher to smoosh it up. Add more water if necessary. Keep it pulpy, but not too wet, like very thick porridge. If you want to speed up the process, put the mixture in a food processor and give it a quick whizz to mush up the paper more finely. When it's a smooth mulch with no bits in it, you're ready for the next step.

**4** Place a towel on your work surface, with a square of parchment paper on top. This bit gets messy – hurray!

*continued*

**Optional**
★ Food processor
★ Knife or cookie
   cutter
★ Food colouring
   or blackberries
★ Flower petals
★ Seeds
★ Small leaves

**5** Lift out a blob of your mixture about the size of a grapefruit. Place it on top of the parchment, cover with a dish towel and squeeze it to get some of the water out of the pulp.

**6** Use your rolling pin to roll out your blob into a flat shape about 3mm (⅛in) thick – you may need to use another sheet of parchment on top of the blob to stop it sticking. If you want to add petals, seeds or small leaves to your paper, scatter them over the pulp as you roll it out. The rolling action will embed them in the paper.

**7** Place a dry dish towel flat on top of the pulp and, using your rolling pin, roll over it to absorb as much water from the paper sheet as you can.

**8** Leave your new piece of paper lying flat on the parchment and find a warm place for it to dry out; this can take days! If you're in a rush, put it in an oven on a low heat to speed things along.

**9** When your paper is dry, use a knife or cookie cutter to trim it or cut it into a cool shape.

## TIP

If you add seeds to the pulp, it becomes magic growing paper! When you're finished with it, place it on top of soil (either in your garden or a flower pot), water it and watch your seedlings sprout.

# Party Hats

AGE: 3+

**No party is complete without a selection of paper hats and making them yourself is so much fun. Cutting, folding and sticking your own hats might even be part of your celebrations.**

Use pretty paper, flashing metallics, disco glitters or powdery pastels if you want to create chic headgear or go low budget and simple by using brown parcel wrap or newspaper. This is where having a good magpie scraps box (see page 11) comes in handy; your tiny beads, snips of fancy ribbon or colourful feathers will all find a home perched on your head.

**Cone Hats**
The easiest hats to make are simple cones. Create high, trumpet-like points or shallower shapes like limpets.

**1** Cut a semi-circle out of your paper. To get a perfectly smooth shape, you could draw halfway around the edge of a large dinner plate.

**2** Roll the semi-circle into a cone shape and use tape, glue or staples to secure it.

**3** Add a spray of tissue paper strips at the top for added pizzazz or a line of pom-poms down the front for a silly clown effect. Glue on a brim to make a witch's hat or add decorations to go with the theme of your party. If you wish, add a length of ribbon to each side of the bottom edge of the hat so that you can tie them under your chin for security.

## YOU'LL NEED

★ Paper
★ Scissors
★ Sticky tape, glue or stapler
★ Fancy bits and pieces – tissue paper, pom-poms, feathers, ribbons, buttons and stickers

## TIP

If you want to make a shallower hat, cut a complete circle and snip a straight line into the centre from the outer edge. Adjust it to the shape you want, and use tape, glue or staples to secure.

# Winged Headband

**AGE: 3+**

The versatile and super-simple nature of headbands means they suit all occasions. It's all about what you choose to deck yours with. You might make a midsummer floral band using pom-pom flowers, like the ones worn by Swedish girls. Or cut out leaf shapes to welcome in harvest time. Perhaps you'll stick bunny ears on yours in spring, a unicorn horn or even a laurel wreath, Greek goddess-style. I've chosen to make these with wings, like a Norse Valkyrie, the god Hermes or, perhaps, goofy Gaul Asterix. Use these instructions as the base for any headband you fancy.

## YOU'LL NEED

★ Paper
★ Scissors
★ Sticky tape, glue or staples
★ Ruler
★ Card

**Optional**

★ Felt-tip pens or coloured pencils
★ Decorations such as flowers, leaves, pom-poms, cut-outs

**1** First, cut your headband strip along the longest edge of your paper. Depending on what you want to stick on it, it should be roughly 5cm (2in) wide. Unless you have a very long piece of paper or a tiny head, you'll probably need to combine two strips to fit.

**2** Using sticky tape, glue or staples, secure the strips at their shortest edges.

**3** Measure the strip around the wearer's head and cut it to fit, allowing an overlap of at least 5cm (2in). Holding the overlap in place, take it off and staple it into a snug-fitting band.

**4** Using the template (see page 172), draw two wings onto paper or card. Remember, you'll need one for the left side and one for the right, so if your paper or card has a pattern with a clear direction, you may need to flip the template over.

**5** If you wish, use a felt-tip pen or coloured pencil to draw feathers onto the wings.

**6** Attach the wings to the headband just behind the wearer's ears. Now put it on and fly!

If your headband is to be highly decorated, it may be easier to glue on your cut-outs or pom-poms before joining the two ends together, but make sure you've marked where the join will be.

# Blooming Flowers

These paper flowers are very easy to make, so you'll have a bowl festooned in blooms in minutes. Young children are transfixed by the gentle unfolding of the petals, which seems almost like magic. Try making them in the evening by candlelight for a calming end to the day.

## YOU'LL NEED

★ Pen or pencil
★ Paper
★ Scissors
★ Bowl of water

**Optional**
★ Felt-tip pens

**1** Use the template (see page 173) to draw flower shapes on to your paper, then cut out your flowers.

**2** Fold in the petals in a circle. They will overlap a little.

**3** Place your flowers on the surface of the water. As the shapes absorb the water, the petals will unfurl.

Try colouring your petals with felt-tip pens and watch the colours fade and smudge, or draw a surprise at the centre, which will only reveal itself as the blooms open.

## TIPS

Why do the flowers unfold? Paper is made up of many tiny wood fibres. As the paper absorbs the water, these fibres expand, flattening out the creases and causing the flowers to bloom. Experiment with different kinds of paper – thick and thin – to find out which kinds take longest to open.

This paper-folding project is a form of origami which dates back many, many centuries (see page 81).

# Rock Jewellery

**Found some beautiful pebbles on your travels? It always seems a shame to throw them away or leave them in a jar on a shelf. Why not show off your favourites and wear them as jewellery?**

## YOU'LL NEED

★ A beautiful small pebble (polished or unpolished) or a piece of sea glass
★ 18–24 gauge wire (craft, garden or electrical wire will all work)
★ Wire cutter or tough scissors
★ Necklace or bracelet chain or leather cord

**Optional**
★ Jewellery safety clasps
★ Pliers

**1** Cut a piece of wire roughly 20cm (8in) long – the length will depend on the size of your rock or pebble.

**2** Wrap it around the stone a few times; you may need to use the pliers for this. Try to create an even, secure 'basket' for your pebble so it won't fall out.

**3** Take the ends of the wire to the top of the pebble and twist them together to keep the rock tightly in place. Leave approximately 2–3cm (1in) of wire at each end.

**4** Take your chain or cut some cord to length (long enough to sit comfortably around your neck and to hook or tie the ends together). Twist the wire ends over it, making a loop, so the pendant is safely threaded onto the cord or chain. Trim the ends of the wire and bend them back on themselves to avoid any sharp edges. If you're using safety clasps for younger children, attach them using pliers.

## TIP

This is a very basic wire wrap. Try using pliers to create swirly patterns, or more intricate spiral shapes for your pebble's 'cage'.

# Interactive Chalk Art

These large-scale drawings allow your kids to dive into new worlds. A space-scape, an underwater adventure or a monster-filled fantasy land – where will you go today? You may be lucky enough to live near a plentiful supply of chalk and find lumps of it on the beach and in the hills near where you live. If not, you may have to buy some.

**YOU'LL NEED**

★ Lots of imagination!
★ Pen and paper
★ Chalk
★ A large tarmac or smooth-paved outdoor space or a sandy beach

**Optional**
★ Dressing-up costumes

**1** Decide what your picture is going to depict (see page 28 for some ideas) and how many kids you want to include. If you have favourite dressing-up outfits, perhaps you might theme your picture around those?

**2** Get together to plan and sketch out your drawing beforehand. Think hard about how it will look when drawn on a large scale and how to fit everyone in. Make sure it's well balanced.

**3** Remember, the picture doesn't have to be complicated; it can be as simple as a bunch of balloons, a winners' podium or a shark's mouth.

**4** Think about where you'd like to create your piece; a large area of dark tarmac works beautifully, but paving, car parks and skateparks work well too (when there are no cars or skaters around!). Beaches need to be sandy and it's best to go as the tide is receding as you'll have more time to work. Bonus points will be awarded if you find somewhere close to a high vantage point such as a bridge, wall or pier, so you can take a great photo of your masterpiece.

**5** Head to your outdoor space and start sketching an outline of how the picture will work with chalk. You might use shoes or other markers to plan out where each part of the drawing will go, but I'm firmly of the opinion that it doesn't really matter and that the wonkier the picture, the funnier it looks.

**6** After you've sketched the outline, give everyone a piece of chalk and let them do their own part of the picture and add their own flourishes.

*continued*

**7** If you're on a beach, use a stick or your finger to draw the picture in a patch of sand. Use stones to outline parts of it, pebbles to decorate, seaweed for trees or hair and driftwood for swords.

**8** Dress up and lie down in your masterpiece. Strike a pose!

**9** Now get someone to go as high up as they can to snap a fantastic photograph.

## NEED SOME INSPIRATION?

Perhaps you'd like to draw...
★ a jungle
★ the ocean bed
★ a zoo
★ a planet full of monsters
★ outer space
★ the pyramids
★ a capital city
★ a scene from a favourite movie

Don't forget to dress up in an appropriate costume!

## NO CHALK?

No problem. Make this paving paint instead.

You'll need
★ Cornflour (cornstarch)
★ Water
★ Food colouring
★ Mixing bowls
★ Brushes

**1** Mix equal parts cornflour (cornstarch) and water, and divide the mixture into separate bowls.

**2** Add as much food colouring as you need to each bowl, stirring well so the colour is evenly mixed.

**3** Use brushes to create your pavement Picasso.

**4** The paint will last a few days, but washes off easily with water or rain.

# Pebble Paperweights

Pebbles are naturally beautiful, but decorating them with scraps of pretty paper (a craft known as decoupage) transforms them into something more personal. Take some of your flattest, most even stones, choose images that say something about you, a friend or relative and create some super-tactile art.

**YOU'LL NEED**

★ Clean, dry pebbles
★ PVA glue
★ Brush
★ Water
★ Scissors
★ Paper image scraps – see tip box for ideas

**Optional**
★ White acrylic paint
★ Clear varnish

**1** If you wish, paint your stones white and leave them to dry. This creates an even, bright background, but if you prefer a natural look, just leave your pebbles unpainted.

**2** Make decoupage glue. You can buy it, but it's expensive, and making your own is so easy. Here's the secret. Water down PVA glue, three parts glue to one part water. If you want to make it glossy, add a little water-based varnish. And that's it!

**3** Carefully cut your scrap to fit your stone. You could use letters cut from newspapers or comics, wrapping paper or paper napkins, or any picture which appeals to you.

**4** Decide where to place your scrap on the stone, then brush the decoupage glue on to the pebble. Place the scrap on the pebble and smooth out any lumps and bumps with your brush, applying glue to the top of the scrap too – take your time over this stage.

**5** Leave the stone to dry. If you wish, apply a coat of varnish.

## TIP

This project is all about the images you choose and how they sit on your pebble. Perhaps you'll find a nautical print or maybe an image of your favourite superhero in your box of comics. You could even find chic, abstract wrapping paper prints to use. These make great presents – why not have a go at creating a personalised paperweight for a friend?

# Clay and Stone Heads

Stones and clay go together like sausages and mash. The natural materials complement each other, the pebbles giving clay texture and interest. Throw in a few sticks and leaves and things look even more fun. Clay is a mineral formed by rocks weathering and breaking down over thousands of years. So I'm claiming it as a kind of stone!

## YOU'LL NEED

★ Air-drying clay
★ Googly or dolls' eyes, or small pebbles and paint
★ Butter or palette knife
★ Small pebbles and jagged stones

**Optional**
★ Twigs
★ Leaves
★ Ferns

**1** Form a piece of clay into a rough face shape.

**2** Use one pinch to form the hollows for eyes and the nose. Keep finessing and tweaking the sockets and profile until you've got it exactly as you want. Press in the eyes. These little faces are all about the eyes, so choose yours wisely. You might use painted pebbles, googly peepers or, as shown in the photo, dolls' eyes.

**3** Use your knife to make a slash for the mouth. Select some stones to use for teeth and poke them into the slash.

**4** Roll little 'sausages' of clay and use them for lips and eyebrows.

**5** Give your face a final shaping and add more stones as ears or tusks.

**6** Add twigs, leaves or ferns to create hair or arms, or hairy arms!

## TIPS

Use air-drying clay for this craft, as stones are more likely to stay in place and sticks and plastic accessories wouldn't survive a firing in a kiln. Alternatively, go organic and use clay you find in a riverbed or claggy estuary.

Make a few clay heads and line them up along your path to welcome (or scare) visitors. Hang one on your bedroom door or put them on a mantelpiece to keep demons away.

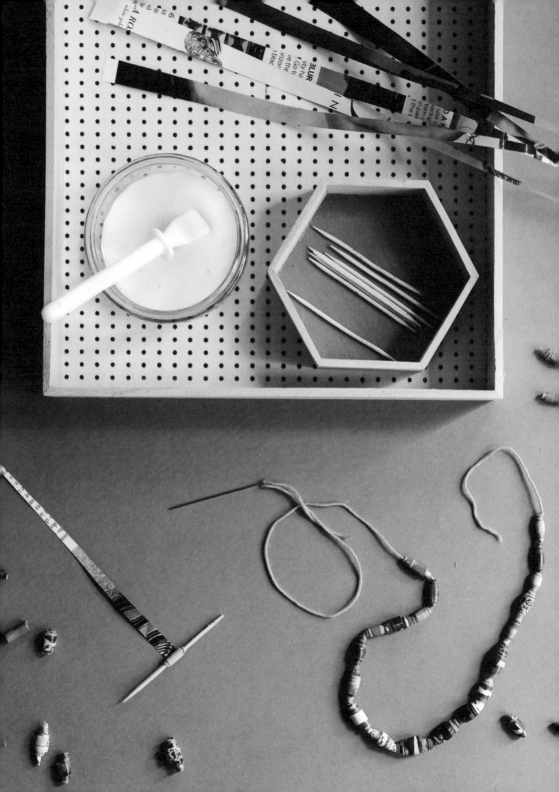

# Magazine Beads

**Popularised in the UK during the Victorian era, more recently paper bead-making has sustained co-operatives in Africa, whose intricately hand-tooled, colourful decorations make for striking jewellery.**

## YOU'LL NEED

★ Colour pages from magazines
★ Scissors
★ Pencil
★ Ruler
★ Paper straws or cocktail sticks (wooden toothpicks)
★ PVA glue
★ Brush or spreader

**Optional**
★ Card
★ Decoupage glue (see page 30 for method)
★ Varnish
★ Needle and embroidery thread (floss) or earring fixings

**1** Cut out the most colourful magazine pages. Using a pencil and ruler, trace very long, equal triangles horizontally or vertically across the page. The base of each should be about 1–1.5cm (¾–⅝in) wide. You might want to make a template out of card to help you or you may brave freehand cutting!

**2** Take the base of the pennant (long triangle) and roll it tightly around a cocktail stick (toothpick) or straw twice.

**3** Dot a little glue down the pennant and keep rolling, keeping the paper tight, until you reach the end. Slide the bead off the stick or straw.

**4** Brush a layer of PVA glue, decoupage glue or varnish over the whole bead. Leave to dry, separated on a plate, tray or suspended on a wire.

**5** String your beads on a length of embroidery thread (floss) to make a necklace or bracelet, or use earring fixings to create dangly designs.

## TIPS

You can paint the beads, but I adore the eye-popping, random colours of magazine pages. Try making them in different shapes, such as a long rectangle or an off-centre triangle template. The beads can be used in so many crafts – to jazz up picture frames, door signs or furniture or create decorations for a Christmas tree.

# Papier-mâché Masks

Papier mâché ('chewed paper' in French) is the most incredible stuff. You can squidge or layer it into any shape you can dream of. It's lightweight, so lends itself to huge creations. It dries hard and is easy to paint in bright colours. Plus it's environmentally friendly.

To build up a shape, you usually layer the paper pulp on an armature or framework. This sounds daunting, but it really isn't. Your frame might be a balloon, a paper bag stuffed with paper or a yogurt pot taped to a cereal box. Sometimes you'll leave the armature in place, sometimes you might remove (or pop) it.

The masks shown overleaf are incredibly simple and made from cardboard with bumps built up from crumpled paper or kitchen foil and masking tape. You could make more elaborate ones using boxes or pots to create a more sculpted armature.

## OTHER IDEAS FOR PAPIER-MÂCHÉ PROJECTS

★ Beads
★ Puppets
★ Hats
★ Boxes
★ Small pieces of furniture
★ Model animals
★ School projects and fancy dress accessories

**For the frame**
★ Cardboard
★ Kitchen foil
★ Masking tape
★ Scissors or craft knife and board

**For the papier mâché**
★ Old newspapers or paper
★ Plain (all-purpose) flour or PVA glue (see pages 40–41)
★ Water

**To decorate**
★ Acrylic or poster paints
★ Brushes
★ Stones
★ Strong glue

**Optional**
★ Ribbons
★ Straw
★ Feathers
★ Buttons
★ Pom-poms

**1** First make your frame. Take your cardboard, mark out and cut an over-sized face shape.

**2** Use pieces of cardboard, foil and masking tape to build up ridges, circles and shapes on your mask. I used art by Picasso and Billy Childish for inspiration. You might look at traditional masks from around the world for more ideas or let your imagination run wild and create your own designs.

**3** Tear your newspaper into strips, roughly 3 x 15cm (1¼ x 6in) or smaller if creating details.

**4** Make up your papier-mâché paste (choose a recipe from pages 40–41).

**5** Dip your strips into the paste and layer them over your ridges, circles and shapes.

**6** Continue building up the layers until you're satisfied with the shape of your mask.

**7** Let your mask dry overnight.

**8** Use paints to decorate your mask. You may choose a muted, monochrome palette or opt for something more colourful.

**9** Stick stones to the mask using strong glue. Add ribbons, straw or feathers if you wish.

Alternatively, you might choose to skip the papier-mâché paste and use a sealing mixture to keep the detail in the mask at the cardboard-only stage. Mix ¼ cup (about 4 tablespoons) of PVA glue with ¼ cup (also about 4 tablespoons) of plaster of Paris and a tablespoon of water. Apply this thick white mixture like paint to give a chalky finish to your mask while retaining the fine lines.

# Papier-mâché Paste

Choose your paste recipe according to the finish and texture you need for each particular project. Using flour and water is eco-friendly, but glue gives a shinier, powder-free finish, creates a slightly stronger structure and is less prone to rot. It's also better for those with gluten allergies. Once you've made your paste, dip strips of torn-up newspaper into it and use them to build up your creation. These recipes make enough for one or two masks, scale them up if you need more.

* Water
* Saucepan
* Plain (all-purpose) white flour
* Whisk or spoon
* Pot or bowl
* Newspaper strips

**The Cooked Recipe**
This is a little stronger and shinier than the No-Cook version. Using a cup to measure your ingredients ensures you get the proportions correct.

**1** Bring 1 cup of water to the boil in a saucepan.

**2** In a bowl, blend ¼ cup of flour with ¼ cup of the water using a whisk or spoon.

**3** Slowly trickle this mixture into the boiling water remaining in the pan.

**4** Keep the pan at a low, rolling boil and whisk the mixture for a few minutes.

**5** Continue until the mixture is thick (like double/heavy cream). Add more flour if it's too thin or pour in a little more water if it's too thick.

**6** Pour into a pot or bowl and let it cool.

**7** Soak your newspaper strips in the mixture and layer them onto whatever you're using as a frame.

★ Plain (all-purpose) white flour
★ Bowl
★ Spoon or whisk
★ Hot water from the tap (faucet)
★ Spoon or whisk
★ Newspaper strips

### The No-Cook Recipe

**1** Add ¼ cup of flour into the bowl.

**2** Slowly add ¼ cup of hot water and stir or whisk.

**3** Keep blending and adding water until it's the consistency of glue. Add more water if it's looking a little thick and more flour if it's looking a little thin.

**4** Soak your newspaper strips in the mixture and layer them on to whatever you're using as a frame.

★ Bowl
★ PVA glue
★ Water
★ Spoon or whisk
★ Newspaper strips

### The Glue Recipe

**1** In your bowl, use your spoon to mix one cup of glue and two cups of cold water.

**2** Soak your newspaper strips in the mixture and layer them on to whatever you're using as a frame.

## PAPIER-MÂCHÉ PULP

Want to add more detail to your mask? Make papier-mâché pulp by soaking newspaper in water overnight, and then shredding it more finely with your fingers or a blender stick. Add flour or glue to the porridge-like mixture to create a clay-like substance that you can use to create details and smooth, fine sculptures.

# Halloween Rocks

**AGE: 3+**

**Spooky but cute, these drop-dead easy designs are fun to create in the build-up to Halloween. They make sweet party gifts or, when piled in a bowl, add to your dread-filled décor. Pick from a petrifying pumpkin, a grisly gravestone, a creepy cat, a ghoulish ghost, a scary skull or a bandaged mummy.**

## YOU'LL NEED

★ Flat, smooth pebbles
★ Acrylic paints in white, black, brown, yellow and orange
★ Brushes

**Optional**
★ Spray primer
★ Acrylic paint pens
★ Varnish

**1** Choose your rocks wisely. You'll need triangle-shaped ones for cats, ovals for the pumpkin designs, jagged slates for headstones, round rocks for mummies, teardrop-shaped pebbles for ghosts and long ovals for the skulls. They should all be as flat as possible.

**2** Wash your rocks and let them dry.

**3** If your rocks are brown or black, paint them with white acrylic paint or, if you're doing a really large batch, spray with white primer.

**4** Select an appropriately shaped rock and give it a base coat of orange or black if needed. Let it dry.

**5** Pick out details on your rock, using our designs to guide you. I like to use acrylic paint pens as their fine lines and steady flow of colour make them perfect for drawing on rocks. However, a thin paintbrush and a steady hand will do just as good a job.

**6** Leave your rocks to dry for an hour or two.

**7** Varnish if you wish.

# Paper Village

**You might spend an afternoon making a village or you might take weeks. Watching it grow, adding new details or creating designs is fascinating. You might use a toy train track as a base or line the streets with model cars. This is a winter scene – the houses look so cosy lit from within and you might even add a sprinkle of flour 'snow'.**

## YOU'LL NEED

★ Paper or card
★ Scissors
★ Glue

**Optional**
★ Felt-tip pens
★ Cellophane (such as see-through sweet/candy wrappers)
★ Battery-powered tea lights
★ Sifted flour

It might seem like a simple idea, but you can be absorbed in creating a paper village, town or city for hours or even days. Start small. Trace the template on pages 170–171 onto paper or card, then fold and glue the tabs in place to make a house.

Make a roof out of a rectangle-shaped piece of card just big enough to hang over the edges of the walls. You can make fancier roofs by cutting scalloped edges and layering smaller scalloped shapes to create a tiled effect.

Then make another, adapting the template to make houses of different heights. Vary the houses by adding doors and windows in different sizes. Now try a school, a shop, an apartment block.

Map out paper streets that echo where you live or go fantastical. Cut out a semi-circle, then snip a line to the centre and secure with glue or tape to make teepee-shaped houses, or design or find templates to make pyramids or dodecahedrons. Cut out trees with little tabs at the bottom to stick to the ground, or flowers, or playgrounds with slides, swings and roundabouts. Make tiny, cone-shaped people (scale down the teepee method) and take them shopping and playing. Create cut-out streams, rivers, boats, factories and docks.

Keep it simple by using brown or white card or thick paper, or add splashes of colour with pens, kitchen foil lakes and cellophane windows. Walk your action figures down the streets or watch them have battles above the rooftops. Drive model cars along the streets. Put battery-powered tea lights inside your buildings as night falls and watch them glow. Dust flour over them for a festive snowfall.

What will your village look like? The only limit is your imagination.

# LEARNING

**Have fun while – shhhhhhhh – learning.
Sneak a little science, maths and reading
into your play using these creative
ways with rocks, paper and scissors.**

# Rock Constellations

AGE: 3+

**Go for a quick zip around the galaxy, but be back in time for tea. Immersing yourself in the constellations is a great way of learning how stars are dotted across the night sky. Make use of a beach day to create your own solar system; this works best on a wide expanse of deserted sand so pick an hour when the shoreline isn't too crowded.**

## YOU'LL NEED

★ Notepad
  and pen or a
  constellation
  chart
★ A large, flat area
  of sand
★ White stones
  or chalk rocks
★ Stick

OR

★ Paved area
★ Pebbles
★ Chalk

**1** Ahead of time, do your research. Find a good astronomy book or look online and jot down the shapes of some basic constellations. In the northern hemisphere I like Orion, Taurus, Scorpius and Ursa Major, or if you're in the southern hemisphere, you might look up Hydra, Crux or Centaurus.

**2** Now head to the beach and gather a pile of white stones or chalk rocks. If you can't find white, any colour will do.

**3** Using your notes, mark out constellations with rocks. Make them as large or as small as you like. You might choose to make a 10m (33ft) Orion or a teeny-tiny Ursa Major.

**4** Use a sharp rock, a stick or your finger to draw lines in the sand joining up the rocks. Constellations are the universe's largest dot-to-dots and you're recreating them!

**5** Now go for a trip around your stars!

## TIP

If you're not near a beach, mark out your constellations on a pavement, concrete or piece of tarmac near you and use chalk lines to join up your stones.

**AGE: 5+**

# Möbius Strips

**Möbius strips are almost laughably simple, yet endlessly fascinating; half magic trick, half physics demonstration. Make one to captivate a small child, create two or three to perform head-scratching feats, or use them as a springboard to explore geometry and to take a leap into infinity.**

**YOU'LL NEED**

★ Ruler
★ Paper
★ Scissors
★ Sticky tape, glue or glue dots

**Optional**
★ Pencil

**1** Cut a strip of paper 2cm (¾in) wide and 10cm (4in) long.

**2** Twist the strip once or any odd number of times, then secure the ends with tape or glue to form a loop.

Slide your finger or use a pencil to draw along the surface of the ring. WHOA! The line you're tracing doesn't stop and extends into infinity. The shape only has one side! This curiosity was discovered in 1858 by German mathematician August Möbius and has fascinated engineers, mathematicians and philosophers ever since. The Dutch artist M. C. Escher was famously obsessed with the shape, sending red ants scuttling along one in his woodcut Möbius Strip II.

## TIP

The fun doesn't stop here. Draw a line down the centre of the strip, then cut along the line. Rather than the two loops you might expect, you'll end up with one giant ring. Take another Möbius strip and try drawing a line about one third of the way up the strip, along the length. Eventually this line will connect with itself. Snip along this line and you'll end up with two, interconnected loops. It's a brain tease!

# The Upside-Down Glass Trick

**'For my next trick, I will keep water in the glass using only a piece of paper (with a little help from air pressure)!' Not only does this incredible illusion demonstrate some Very Serious Science Stuff, it also makes a cold and wet prank.**

YOU'LL NEED

★ Piece of thick paper, card, laminated paper (such as a glossy magazine cover) or an old playing card
★ Scissors
★ Glass or plastic beaker
★ Water

**1** Cut the paper just large enough to cover the top of the glass.

**2** Fill the glass to the very top with water.

**3** Cover the mouth of the glass with the paper.

**4** This is the tricky bit so you might want to practise over a sink or bath as it can take a few goes to get it right. Keeping your hand on top of the paper, turn the glass upside down.

**5** Take your hand away. A little will leak out, but the water should stay in place.

**6** Invite a friend or enemy to pull the paper away.

## TIP

How does it work? Well, it's mostly to do with air pressure. All around us, molecules of air are constantly colliding with objects, the ground and us. When you fill the glass almost to the top and a little bit of water leaks out, it creates a pocket of air at the top of the glass, which is at a lower pressure than the outside. So the air below pushes up on the card with enough force to keep the water in. In addition, the surface tension of the water helps to keep the card fixed in place. Try experimenting with different sized cups, thicknesses of paper and liquids.

# Building Blocks

There's something jaw-dropping about taking a two-dimensional piece of paper and turning it into something spectacular. Spending an afternoon creating your own building blocks and then using them to create superstructures is deeply satisfying and even, shhh, teaches kids about strengths, forces, design and engineering.

Spend half an hour or so making a selection of blocks. I've given you instructions for making triangles, but you might like to adapt them to fold basic cubes, cylinders, pyramids and rectangular prisms. Keep the lengths of your shapes' sides the same to create a modular system. Open-sided designs are more stylish and easier for little fingers to hold.

## YOU'LL NEED

★ Heavyish gauge paper (white paper is fine, but coloured is so much prettier)
★ Ruler
★ Pencil
★ Scissors
★ Sticky tape

### Optional
★ Guillotine or craft knife and cutting board

**Tumbling Triangles**

**1** Use a ruler and pencil to mark out strips 9cm (3¾in) x 3cm (1¼in), and cut them out.

**2** Use a ruler and scissors to score (use the tip of the blade to mark the paper but don't cut through it) lines horizontally across your strips at 3cm (1¼in) and 6cm (2½in). If you've got a guillotine or craft knife and cutting board, use those for a sharper edge, but, as ever, beware of small fingers meeting sharp blades.

**3** Fold the strips at the scored lines to create a triangle shape and secure at the top with a piece of tape. Repeat until you have at least 20 triangles.

**4** Cut some 3cm (1¼in) x 8–15cm (3¼–6in) strips to serve as horizontal beams.

*continued*

**5** Create a structure by balancing the triangles and beams. You might try making a square or triangle shape, or perhaps even a bridge. Try resting objects on the beams to find out just how strong your creation is. Or you can omit the beams and try stacking the triangles on their own.

Expand your selection of shapes and build tube-shaped pieces and square blocks, or experiment with materials – see how card, corrugated cardboard and thinner paper work. You might try making cylinders and cutting slits in them so they slot together. Or play with scale, making much bigger blocks.

**The Building Game**
If your children are a little older, set them a challenge. Split them into teams or get them to play individually. Give them a pad of heavy stock coloured paper, scissors and tape, and ask them to make the tallest structure they can in half an hour. Vary it up by giving them different kinds of paper such as newspaper, card and, if you really want to give them a tough nut to crack, wrapping paper!

# Alphabet Rocks

Creating a set of tactile letter rocks makes learning letters and making words fun. You can tailor this to your strengths. A whizz at painting? Use acrylics. Prefer pens? Get out the Sharpies. Love unusual fonts seen in magazines? Cut and paste away! Involve your family as forming letters helps reinforce their shapes and a child's handwritten stone makes a sweet keepsake.

## YOU'LL NEED

★ At least 26 smallish pebbles
★ Selection of magazines and comics or wrapping paper
★ PVA glue
★ Paint, felt-tip pens or rub-on transfer letters or stickers

**Optional**
★ Pretty bag for storing the stones

**1** Wash and dry your 26 stones.

**2** If you want to be fancy, use a different colour stone for vowels. Paint, draw, stick or rub a single letter onto each one. If you're cutting letters out of magazines and decoupaging (sticking them onto the stones), follow the instructions on page 30. Find different fonts and interestingly shaped letters in the newspapers, comics or magazines you have to hand or cut the shapes of letters out of nicely patterned wrapping paper.

**3** Add in punctuation if you wish, such as exclamation marks, commas and speech marks. Or do an upper and lower case set. If you need to form longer words, add letter doubles – use a Scrabble set to work out how letters should be distributed.

**4** Use diluted PVA glue (see page 30) to seal and add shine to your stones.

You might like to theme your stones. Cut out letters from your favourite comic or magazine, or use a limited paint palette. If using rub-down transfers, pick fonts from your favourite era – medieval, Victorian or my personal go-to decade, the 1970s!

### TIP

Alphabet rocks make a good basis for signs and warnings. Why not stick some to driftwood and make a name plaque for your bedroom door. Or your house's name or number?

WEAR
PROTECTIVE
CLOTHING
AND SAFETY
GOGGLES

# Identifying Rocks

**Rocks come in endless varieties, shapes and colours. Being able to identify stones you find on a beach, in a cave, by a lake or just on the ground is a superpower rather like birdwatching or flower spotting. It will take time and patience to be able to name a rock with certainty, but it's worth putting in the hours as it's an impressive skill.**

### Pebble Identifier

Geologists have names for the three types of stones you'll commonly find: sedimentary, metamorphic and igneous. Grab a handful and see if you can work out which types you've picked up, or look up at the surrounding mountains, cliffs and huge rocks and try to work out what they're made of. It's worth getting a cheap rock-spotting guidebook or finding a good app to help you figure out what you're looking at.

### Sedimentary

These are layered rocks formed as particles of minerals, animals and plants have settled over thousands and thousands of years on the bed of a body of water, and which harden as the water recedes. You might be able to spot these layers in your pebble. Look closely for lines or check to see if bits come away if you gently rub the stone; these rocks are often soft and grainy. You might even be lucky enough to find a fossil embedded in these kind of rocks. Examples of sedimentary rocks include sandstone, limestone and shale.

### Metamorphic

Metamorphic rocks started out as sedimentary stones, but were transformed and compacted by intense heat or enormous pressure – or both – into hard, crystalline masses. You may be able to spot the layers in these tougher rocks; this sub-group is called foliated metamorphic rocks, while rocks without layers are called non-foliated. Examples of metamorphic rocks include slate, marble, gneiss, lapis lazuli, anthracite and schist.

**Igneous**

Formed from hot, molten lava that has cooled, crystallized and solidified, igneous rocks are super hard! They are mostly crystalline and very hard to break. There are two main categories of these rocks: extrusive and intrusive. Extrusive rocks form on the surface of the earth and cool quickly. Some, such as obsidian, are glossy and have cooled very speedily; they contain no crystals. Intrusive rocks are formed more slowly beneath the surface of the earth and the longer process allows crystals to form; this produces speckled rocks with flashes of crystalline brilliance, such as granite. Other examples of igneous rocks include basalt, pumice and gabbro.

It's often easier to identify a pebble if you wet it first as this makes the colours sing and become more distinct. Try gently scratching the stone with a coin to see if it leaves a mark. Run your stone over a hard surface and see if a line or streak appears; what colour is it? If you have safety goggles, you might try to break apart the stone to see what's inside it. Is it crystalline? Rough or smooth? Try using a magnet to see if it's attracted.

Different regions are renowned for particular minerals or stone. You might find black jet, orange amber, quartz, chalk, flint or blood-red garnets on a beach near you; some stones are much rarer than others and finding them is like discovering treasure.

## TIP

Remember, never take stones from a beach. The occasional small pebble or rock might seem fine, but pocketing them means you risk destroying habitats and causing the shoreline to erode or disappear. Taking stones is even illegal on some beaches, so it's best to admire stones and rocks where they are; maybe snap a picture of your find, as if you were on a stone safari. Perhaps practise offsetting; for every stone you put in your pocket, take and recycle five pieces of plastic or rubbish. If you're really keen to collect stones, buy them online from ethical, reputable stores.

# Chromatography and Rainbow Flowers

**Scientists use a process called chromatography to separate a mixture and find out what it is made up of. Here you're using a basic version of the method to discover what individual hues are blended to make coloured pen inks.**

### YOU'LL NEED

★ White coffee filters
★ Felt-tip pens and non-permanent markers
★ Small glasses or cups (shot glasses work brilliantly)
★ Water
★ Large glasses or cups

**Optional**
★ Scissors
★ Pipe cleaners

**1** Using a pen, draw a ring about 5cm (2in) in diameter in the centre of the filter. On some designs, you might find it easier to trace the line where the filter's plain inner circle meets the ridged part.

**2** If the filter isn't pre-folded, fold it in half and then in half again, and crease.

**3** Fill the small glass with 2–5cm (¾–2in) of water.

**4** Pop your filter into the water, pointed side downwards; the pen circle should be well above the waterline.

**5** Wait a few minutes to let the water creep up the filter so it's absorbed into the paper. It will reach the circle. Bam! Do you see the colours separating? Let the water continue to travel up the filter, taking the different dyes in the ink with it. Be patient. When you're happy with the result, pull your filter out.

**6** Repeat the experiment with a new coffee filter, using different pens to find your favourite effect. Some pens will give a one-colour tie-dye style, others will separate out into a rainbow of different colours. I find that black pens give the most spectacular, multi-hued result.

**7** Let your filters dry (pop them in bigger cups to stop them sticking to any surfaces), then try crafting using your colourful circles. Fold them into eighths and use scissors to snip them into snowflakes, or create butterflies or flowers by twisting them in half and securing with pipe cleaners.

# Flint Knapping

**AGE: 7+,**
**adult supervision**
**is essential**

WEAR
PROTECTIVE
CLOTHING
AND SAFETY
GOGGLES

For thousands of years, humans made tools and weapons out of rocks. We tend to think of Stone Age tools as being unsophisticated, but ancient people were highly skilled in the art – called 'knapping' – of making arrowheads, knives and peelers. You're going to make a sharp-edged arrowhead out of a simple stone you can pick up on the street. If you're worried about safety, find a flint-knapping course or workshop at a museum near you that teaches the technique.

Important: anyone knapping stones, or who is nearby must, must, must wear protective clothing and safety goggles. There will be fragments of stone flying around and they are dangerous. Keep really small children well out of the way and always work outside. Make sure you sweep up carefully afterwards, as there will be shards of stone on the ground. Although knapping is traditionally done in your lap, it's much safer to use the ground or a very tough table or workbench. Always do this under adult supervision.

YOU'LL
NEED

★ 2 hard, fine-grained rocks, such as flint, chert, agate, obsidian or jasper.
  These stones fracture easily, but are tough enough to keep a sharp edge.
  They should be fairly large – at least the size of your fist.

**Essential**
★ Safety goggles (conventional glasses are not adequate protection)
★ Gardening gloves
★ Long-sleeved tops and long trousers
★ Hat

**Optional**
★ Hammer
★ Vice

## Make an Arrowhead

**1** Put on your safety goggles and protective clothes. No protection, no knapping!

**2** There are two methods to knapping stone: percussion flaking, which takes off big chunks, and pressure flaking, which is used to refine edges and for more subtle shaping.

**3** First try percussion flaking. You will probably be starting with a large chunk of stone or 'core'.

**4** Put your stone on the floor or in your vice and strike it with a hammer or your other stone. It may take a few blows, but eventually it will split into flakes. Be careful of the sharp edges.

**5** Take a 7–20cm (2¾–8in) flake and hit the stone more gently around its edges to form the arrowhead shape. Experiment with angles to find the most effective way to strike the piece.

**6** Keep trimming and striking until you have a piece a little larger than your intended result.

**7** Grind the edges of your stone against a hard, rough surface such as a paving slab or road to remove all the fragile edges.

**8** When you're happy with this rough shape, use your other stone or a hammer to press into the edges; don't hit, just apply pressure. The edges should flake away and sharpen. Use this technique to make fine adjustments to the shape and construct its final form.

**9** Be aware that this arrowhead is sharp and dangerous. Keep it safely tucked away and never go out with it.

Use your flint to transport you back in time and connect you directly with the past. Imagine what it would have been like to have one of these as your primary tool for cutting vegetables, meat or for use in construction. Try yours out in similar ways!

# Sundials

**AGE: 4+**

Before phones, before digital watches, before clockwork, people used the sun to tell the time. And you can too! You can make a sundial in many ways, but this is a super-simple method. Make a temporary time-teller over a long, lazy day at the beach, or create a more permanent one in your back garden, on a balcony or in your nearest green space.

## YOU'LL NEED

★ 12 pebbles
★ A sunny day and plenty of time
★ Stick
★ Something to tell the time – a watch or phone will do
★ Compass or phone app to tell you which way north or south lie

**Optional**
★ Pen or chalk

**1** If you wish, mark your pebbles from 1–12 using pen or chalk.

**2** Start making your sundial after the sun has risen. It's best to do this on a bright, cloud-free day for sharp, consistent shadows.

**3** Poke your stick into the ground, slanted towards the north if you're in the northern hemisphere, and if you're in the southern hemisphere, slant it south. Use a compass or phone app to determine where north (or south) is. The stick is your 'gnomon' – what a great word – that casts a shadow.

**4** As an hour turns, place a pebble (marked with the appropriate time) where the stick's shadow falls.

**5** Return after an hour and repeat, continuing until the sun sets.

**6** Use the stick's shadow to tell the time.

## FUN FACT

As the earth rotates, the sun appears to track across the sky. As it arcs, it causes objects to cast shadows. These shadows move in a clockwise direction (anti-clockwise in the southern hemisphere). It takes the sun four minutes to appear to move one degree in the sky, so an hour on the sundial is 15 degrees. Your sundial is rudimentary so it cannot allow for adjustments like summertime, or, of course, tell you the time after the sun has gone down.

# Fossil Hunting

All this hunting for stones and rocks means you may well find a fossil or two. Fossils are the remains of creatures and plants that lived on the earth millions of years ago. They form when an animal or plant dies or falls to the floor. Layers of sand and silt slowly build up around the creature or vegetation and harden into sedimentary rock (see page 59). The organic bones or leaves are replaced by minerals from water that seeps into the rock. These minerals create an exact, rock-hard copy of the original bones, shell, plant, or even dinosaur poo.

You can find fossils anywhere: beaches, quarries, cliffs or rivers – any area heavy with sedimentary rocks. It's definitely not necessary to hammer away and damage cliffs to find them. Try turning over rocks and pebbles below soft cliffs to look for the telltale ridges and shapes of fossils. There will be lots around after a big storm, although you must be careful never to hang out under dangerous crumbling edges or precarious overhangs. Move slowly, be patient and keep looking. Fossil hunting is all about spending lots of time searching. Some fossils are in rocks way too big to pick up, so take a photo and leave them be.

Fossils to look out for include:

**Ammonites**
One of the easiest fossils to spot, ammonites look like flat, spiral-like snail shells and are the remains of a tentacled, squid-like sea creature. Some are teeny-tiny, others as big as a human being!

**Belemnites**
These bullet-shaped fossils are formed from the skeleton of a ten-armed, squid-like creature. The fossils you'll find are part of its tail.

### Sea Urchins
Sea urchin fossils usually look like flattened globes, heart shapes or discs, sometimes with a star pattern on their surface. You may find them in flints that have been embedded in chalky rocks, or just disguised as a round pebble.

### Shark's Teeth
Sharp and pointy, with a strip of root across the bottom, shark's teeth are a pretty common fossil. Some can be as big as your palm!

### Plants
Find fronds and fern shapes on the surface of rocks.

### Seashells
Many fossils are the hardened relatives of the shells you'll find on most beaches. They might look like cockles, clams or oysters.

### Dinosaur Skeletons
Well, who knows what you might find? Keep an eye out for large bone-like rocks, and one day you might strike lucky. In 2015, South African shepherd Dumangwe Thyobeka stumbled on some large pieces of fossilised bone and his discoveries led to the excavation of a huge dinosaur graveyard. Perhaps one day you might find something similar? Discoveries are named by the person who discovered them, so think up some good titles.

## TIPS

★ Remember, never, ever climb up dangerous cliffs or lurk underneath them.
★ Be aware of tides and don't get cut off.
★ Some beaches don't allow fossil hunting, so find out the rules beforehand.
★ Don't pull rocks down or hammer away at them as this can lead to coastal erosion. Be patient and let the fossils come to you.
★ Never take too many fossils from a beach. Be sparing.

CHAPTER
THREE

# OUT AND ABOUT

Spending a sunny day at the beach,
in the country or heading to a park?
These ideas require minimal preparation,
and will make your time in the open air
even more fun. In colder seasons,
they'll act as a spur to get you all
out of the house.

# Stone Skimming

**The art of lazily throwing a stone across a still body of water and watching it skip across the surface is something every child should master. However, making it look easy will take a little practice.**

## YOU'LL NEED

★ Calm stretch of water – the dream is a mirror-like millpond just around sunset
★ Stone – pick yours with care. Look for the flattest, smoothest one you can find. It should fit neatly into the palm of your hand and weigh about the same as a tennis ball

**1** Using your usual throwing arm, make a U shape with your thumb and forefinger, and balance the stone on the side of your middle finger.

**2** You're aiming to ensure the stone hits the water at the shallowest possible angle, so get down as low as you can.

**3** Pull your arm back, then propel the stone towards the water in a straight, flat, even line. As you release it from your hand, flick it against your first finger to give it a bit of spin. It should travel in a horizontal line and hop off the water's surface.

**4** Count the bounces!

## TIPS

Hurling stones about can be dangerous. Never, ever throw one if anyone is standing in front of you. Skimming in turns keeps things safer.

Not having any success with stone throwing? A very satisfying variant is to make a catapult and use it to ping your stones into the water.

AGE: 4+

# Noughts and Crosses

**Creating an instant, absorbing game out of almost nothing is close to magic and days at the beach are made more fun with giant noughts and crosses. Of course, you can scratch games in the sand, but they feel so much classier played with rocks.**

### YOU'LL NEED

★ 5 evenly shaped stones of one colour
★ 5 evenly shaped stones of another colour

**Optional**
★ Driftwood, shells or seaweed

**1** Mark out a grid. You can use a stick or your finger to draw in the sand, or use seaweed, driftwood or shells to mark out lines.

**2** Choose which colour pieces you'd like to play.

**3** Take turns in placing them, the first player to make a line wins.

If you're in the countryside or a park, use sticks to mark out your board, try chalk on a paved area, or 'paint' a board in your garden using watered-down mud. Experiment using different materials and whatever you have lying around.

If you want more of a challenge, mark out an 8 x 8 board, gather 24 stones in two different colours and play draughts or checkers. You might even try to find enough appropriately shaped and coloured stones to attempt chess!

## TIP

Scale things down and make little portable noughts and crosses, dominos, draughts or chess sets out of stones. Find small, flattish pebbles of equal sizes in two colours, wash and dry them, then use acrylic paint to mark Xs and Os, domino dots, numbers, pictures or symbols to represent chess pieces, and varnish if required. Mark out the grid using a pen on a sheet of paper, make one from twigs or driftwood, weave paper to create a chequerboard or use an existing one from your games cupboard. Keep your play stones in a drawstring bag.

# Paper Water Bombs

**AGE: 4+**

**Shop-bought balloon water bombs are pricey and a disaster for the environment. Why not make your own from paper? Once you know this trick, you'll be able to rustle some up at a moment's notice – surely an essential life skill! The step-by-step photos on the following pages will help you with the paper folding.**

## YOU'LL NEED

★ Paper
★ Scissors
★ Water

**1** Cut your paper into a square.

**2** Fold it in half to create a rectangle, crease hard, then open. Turn the paper 90 degrees and fold into another rectangle, crease hard and open out again.

**3** Fold it in half to create a triangle, crease hard, then open. Turn the paper 90 degrees and fold into another triangle, crease hard and open out again.

**4** Lay the paper flat in front of you, pinch on the diagonal lines and push in towards the centre. This will make the paper stand up in the centre.

**5** Push the paper flat to form a triangle. Fold up the corners of the triangle to the top, turn over and repeat. You should now have a diamond shape.

**6** Fold in the sides of the diamond, turn over and repeat.

**7** Poke your finger into the the little 'pockets' you have just created to gently open them out a little.

**8** Fold down the four little 'tabs' at the top and bottom of the shape and secure them in the pockets. Turn over and repeat.

**9** Gently blow into the little hole at the top of the balloon to inflate it. Fill with water and have fun! Watch out, suckers!

STEPS
1–3

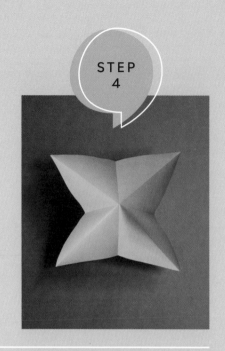

STEP
4

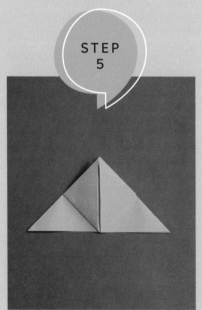

STEP
5

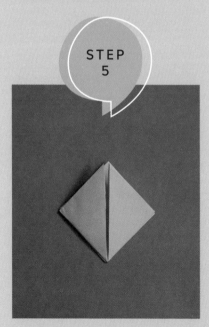

STEP
5

78

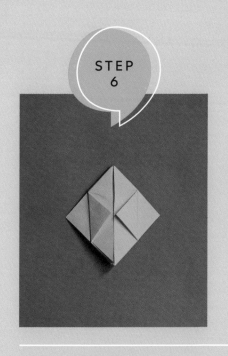

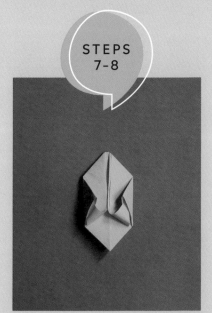

## FUN FACT

The water bomb is a classic origami model. Origami, or the art of paper folding, is an East Asian tradition, which followed the invention of paper around the second century AD or possibly even earlier. It became hugely popular in Japan around AD 500 when Buddhist monks introduced paper to the country. By the 1600s, the whole of Europe was entranced by the craft. It's a meditative, creative, art form, with beautiful results and it hones fine motor skills. Skilled origami devotees can conjure up animals, houses, people and whole worlds from single, flat sheets of paper. And you thought this was all about giving a friend a cold, wet surprise!

# Land Art

AGE: 3+

**Land art uses the landscape around us as a gallery and first became popular in the west during the 1960s and 1970s. Large-scale pieces include huge earthworks, natural stone sculptures, woven branches or formations created with rocks that, over time, become slick with green algae, such as Robert Smithson's Spiral Jetty in the USA or the Forest of Dean Sculpture Trail in the UK. There are humbler creations, too. Contemporary land artists might create tiny transparent leaf boxes filled with seeds, mandalas combed into the beach, rocks embossed with colourful leaves, or simple stone circles where the colours of the pebbles flow into each other like a rainbow.**

Why not try making some land art on a walk in the country or at the beach? You might like to plan your project beforehand using sketches, or search online for inspiration. Or go freeform and be inspired by the pieces of stone, shell and pebble you find when you're out. Be led by the colour and shape of the stones you find. Sort them into groups according to their appearance, then lay them flat to make a spiral, circle, square, butterfly, animal or mandala pattern. Place them on sand or a clear piece of ground, or use contrasting rocks to form a 'background' on the beach. You might find a piece of driftwood and balance stones along it. Or place pretty rocks on a groyne or larger rock. Pieces don't have to be large. Smaller children can make faces, figures or animals, adding seaweed or grass for hair. Use a stick to draw lines in the sand or earth to create backgrounds.

Take a picture, then return the rocks to where you found them or, if they're below the tideline, let the sea take them back.

## TIP

Some people think that land art is destructive and in direct opposition to the 'leave no trace' mantra of wilderness lovers. However, land artists say that it promotes awareness of the delicate ecological system and shows that it needs protecting. Be aware of your environment and always follow the rules on page 13.

## TIP

This game may be a little tricky for younger children. The 'snail' version is good for those too young to catch well and will school little gonggi fans in how each round works. Rather than throwing stones into the air, players sweep their hands across the ground to grab their pebbles.

# Gonggi

AGE: 6+

**Gonggi is a traditional Korean game, with versions played across Nepal and southern India. Although you can buy colourful plastic sets of 'stones', it was originally played using pebbles. Practise alone or challenge friends to a match; the more you play, the better you'll become.**

YOU'LL NEED

★ Any number of players
★ 5 or more grape-sized pebbles. You might want to look for some satisfyingly shaped stones and decorate them to create a set for your personal use, or just pick up whatever small rocks are around.
★ Flat surface

The game is about throwing and catching stones in increasingly difficult ways. There are different rounds of the game and many variations on the rules, but let's go with these. Throw five pebbles into the air and catch as many as you can on the back of your hand. The player who lands most is the first to play.

**1** Gently throw your five pebbles or 'gonggi' on the ground.

**2** Pick up one pebble and throw it into the air. While it's in the air, pick up another pebble from the ground. Catch the first stone before it hits the ground. Repeat, keeping the stones in your hand, until all the pieces are picked up.

**3** Do the whole thing again, but this time picking up two stones (then another and, finally, one), then three (then another two), then all four at once. If you've completed all the rounds successfully, you can then score some points.

**4** To score, toss the stones into the air, then flip your hand. Catch as many as you can on the back of your hand.

**5** From the back of your hand, throw them in the air and try to catch as many as you can. The number of stones you catch totals your score for the match.

**6** If you want to show off in the last round, clap your hands before catching the stones or, in one move, try catching stones conventionally and on the back of your hand before they hit the floor. Both these flashy moves will net you double points.

If you make a mistake or a stone hits the ground, the next player takes over and you forfeit your points. The winner is the person with the most points after a pre-determined number of rounds.

# Paper Boats

Making a flotilla of tiny paper boats and sailing them downstream is a traditional, wholesome-feeling pastime. There's something very satisfying for children in folding a three-dimensional shape from paper and then watching their craft set off bravely on a tiny voyage. It's an early lesson in the power of engineering, of art, and of hope and optimism. Folding boats might seem a little complicated, but once you get the hang of pulling the sides out to create a new shape, it's so easy. You'll be making dozens of small ships in no time at all.

## YOU'LL NEED

★ Rectangular sheet of paper, approximately 21 x 30cm (8¼ x 12in, or A4 size)

**1** Set your paper vertically (portrait) in front of you and fold it in half lengthwise (see the step-by-step photos on the following pages). Open it out.

**2** Place the paper horizontally (landscape) and fold it in half, with the crease at the top.

**3** Fold the top corners downwards to meet in the middle.

**4** Fold the bottom, rectangular-shaped part of the paper upwards on each side. You should now have a hat-shaped construction.

**5** Hold the two midpoints of the hat's bottom sides and pull them apart to form a square. Tuck the flaps under each other and flatten.

**6** Fold up the bottom corners to create another, smaller hat shape.

**7** Again, pull out the two midpoints of the bottom side to form a square and flatten.

**8** Grab the two top points and gently pull out to form a boat.

Take them to a park or the seaside and sail away. Make sure that you take them out of the water when you've finished and recycle them. Good sailors keep the seas clean.

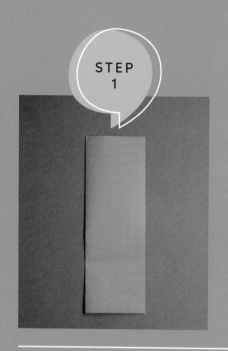

**STEP 1**

**STEP 2**

**STEP 3**

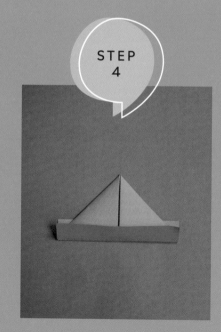

**STEP 4**

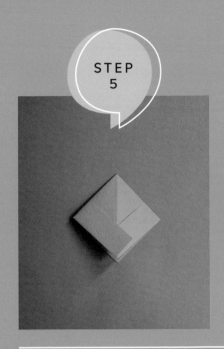

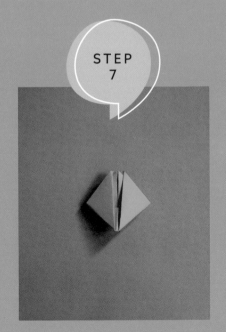

# Positivity Rocks

Positivity does rock! So why not paint some positivity by leaving happy messages for others to find? The rock painting craze is believed to have been started by Megan Murphy from Cape Cod, USA. Her parents had died when she was in her early twenties and she loved to look for signs in nature from them on her beach walks. From this sprung her idea of leaving positive messages on rocks and leaving them for others to find.

Now thousands of people do the same across the world; you may even have picked up a stone with a cheery picture or motto yourself. Some of the stones have social media hashtags or group addresses on the back, others are just cast into the ether for whoever needs them. Why not make a habit of creating positivity rocks and leaving them for others to find?

**YOU'LL NEED**

★ Good-sized, clean, flat stones
★ Acrylic paint and brushes or marker pens

**Optional**
★ Soft pencil
★ Varnish or clear nail polish

**1** Hold your stones and think positive thoughts. Try to transfer all those good vibes to the rock you're holding!

**2** Choose your pattern, picture, slogan or quote. You might choose to draw a cheery picture, an emoji or a drawing that represents something positive, such as a bee (the power of community), butterfly (rebirth), cat (magic), swallow (hope), sun (life and plenty), moon (female power). Or a quote from your favourite book, a line from a movie or play. Or a single word, written beautifully: 'love', 'hope', 'faith', 'smile', 'cool', 'happy'.

**3** If you like, sketch out your design on your stone using a soft pencil or go freestyle.

**4** Paint your design or use marker pens to ink it onto the stone. If you want to make your stone weatherproof, seal it with varnish or clear nail polish.

**5** Head out and leave your stone somewhere exciting – on top of a wall, on a bench, at a bus-stop, in a waiting room, in a park, on a café table, on a friend's doorstep (a great birthday gift).

# Stainbows

AGE: 3+

ADULT
SUPERVISION IS
RECOMMENDED

The natural world is packed with bright, vibrant hues. Celebrate and explore its diversity by playing a game and making art at the same time. Red, orange, yellow, green, blue, indigo, violet - all the colours of the stainbow. This activity works in any outdoor setting and is fun for all ages, although very young children will need adult supervision.

**YOU'LL NEED**

★ Sheet of white paper for each player
★ Pen or pencil
★ Timer (or use a stopwatch on your phone)

**1** Sketch out a rainbow with seven stripes on everyone's piece of paper. You may need to label the colours for younger children. No pencil? No worries, you can go freestyle!

**2** The aim of the game is to forage and find natural materials of all colours and rub them on the appropriate spot on the paper to form a rainbow.

**3** Don't worry about filling up the stripes completely, as some colours are in short supply - a small spot still counts.

**4** You might like to set some ground rules. Perhaps avoid picking wild flowers, only take a small petal from those growing in abundance, no use of animals, and make clear if there's anywhere out of bounds.

**5** Set a timer for 15–20 minutes and send everyone out to create their stainbow. Blues, violets and purples are perhaps the trickiest colours to find, but berries and flowers are your friends here. Don't be afraid to get a bit grubby.

**6** When the timer finishes, bring everyone back and have an exhibition. The person who has found the colours closest to a real rainbow wins the pot of gold.

**Colouring Your Stainbow**
Flower petals, soft rocks, mud, seaweeds , vegetables, bark and sticks, moss, grasses, leaves, berries, fruit, mushrooms. Make sure you tell children not to eat berries (apart from common ones like strawberries) or mushrooms - as some may be poisonous - and ensure they wash their hands after the game.

# Spoof

Usually played with coins, this game is just as much fun with pebbles. Spoof might be won through skill and judgement, but guessing works too, which means the youngest members of the family have a chance to win. It's a good game to play if you're trying to work out who is going to do a particular chore, such as washing the camp's dirty plates or going to collect ice creams.

The game might seem simple, but there are strategies to be discovered, poker faces to be pulled and a huge amount of fun to be had.

### YOU'LL NEED

★ Any number of players
★ 3 very small pebbles for each player

**1** Spoof is played in a series of rounds. Players hide up to three stones in one of their hands, and the aim of the game is to guess how many stones are held in total by all players.

**2** Round one: stand in a circle. Each player hides any number of stones, from zero to three, in one of their hands.

**3** The oldest player plays first. They guess how many stones are, in total, in everyone's hands.

**4** Going clockwise, the next player does the same, and so on round the circle. You may not call a number that's already been given.

**5** When everyone's given a guess, all players open their hands to reveal the total number of stones in play.

**6** The player who has called the correct number sits down.

**7** Round two: exactly the same as the first round, but the next player next to the one who has sat down is the first to call.

**8** Last person left standing loses. They must do the washing up, collect the ice creams or just get laughed at.

# Labyrinths and Mazes

Labyrinths are a kind of maze, but a maze with only one path in and one path out. There is no puzzle to be solved and no dead-end alleys. Many people believe that walking labyrinths calms and soothes them. Labyrinths are used as a basis for rituals and, in some cases, to promote mindfulness. Why not spend a few hours building your own? If you're lucky enough to have a large garden it might be a permanent fixture, or make a temporary creation in a field or on a beach.

According to mythology, the original labyrinth was commissioned by King Minos of Crete and built at Knossos by Daedalus. It housed the Minotaur, a creature with the body of a man and the head of a bull. Theseus bravely entered the twisting passages to slay the beast, but almost got lost in the intricate pathways. You'll find images of labyrinths scattered across Greek and Roman art and mosaics. There are also labyrinths in Native American, Indian, South American, Scandinavian and Egyptian cultures.

YOU'LL NEED

★ Stones or pebbles – lots of them, lots and lots. Preferably of similar size and colour, but that isn't too important.

This labyrinth is a very basic version of the Cretan pattern. You're building a small one using a 3 x 3 grid. The classical design has seven circuits, so if you want to build that, your starting grid needs to be a 5 x 5 square.

**1** Arrange nine pebbles in a 3 x 3 square. It can be as large or small as you want, but 30cm (12in) between each stone is probably the absolute minimum; the bigger the better! Number your stones in your head 1–9, working left to right.

**2** Using your stones to form lines and, with the middle pebble as your centre point, create a cross. So stones 2 and 8 are joined by a line, as are stones 4 and 6 (see the step-by-step photos on pages 98–99).

*continued*

**3** Use your stones to form a semicircle line that arches upwards joining stones 2 and 3, creating a shape jutting from the top of the cross like the top of a walking stick.

**4** Create an arc forming an even path from stone 1 to stone 6.

**5** Create another line which arcs over the other paths, from stone 4 to stone 9.

**6** Your last line should start at stone 7, tracing over the top of the other lines, leaving a clear path, and ending up at stone 8.

**7** Your labyrinth is complete!

It's believed labyrinths were used across cultures for ritual dances as well as representing a symbolic form of pilgrimage. Perhaps you might trace the lines and paths in different ways. Try walking slowly along them in fairy steps, or hopping. Once you reach the centre, think about the path you took to get there and slowly retrace your steps. Try walking backwards. Perhaps you might close your eyes and try to walk the path that way.

Some people write down their troubles or worries on a piece of paper and slowly walk the labyrinth to the centre. When they get there, they rip up the paper and let their troubles float away, then they put the torn pieces of paper into their pocket. As they walk out, they concentrate on all the good things in their life and how much better they feel!

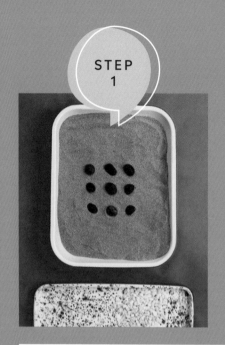

**STEP 1**

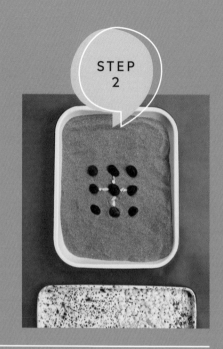

**STEP 2**

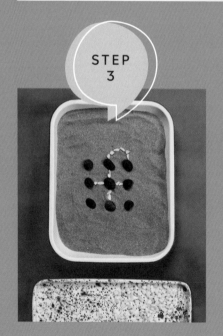

**STEP 3**

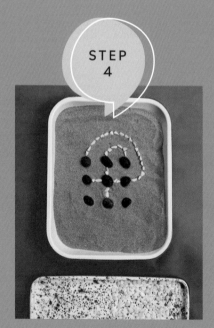

**STEP 4**

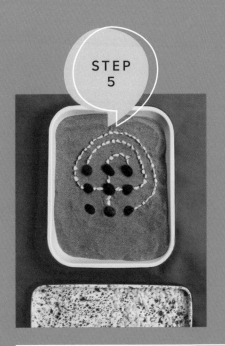

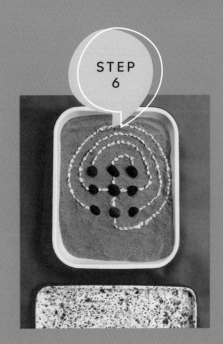

# TIP

Not got enough stones? Or a big enough outdoor space? Try using tiny pebbles to make a mini labyrinth for your action figures or dolls, or to walk with your fingers. Or trace one using a pen on paper.

**AGE: 3+**

# Pebble Stacking

**Meditative and artful, balancing pebbles is an art that celebrates the natural world. There are so many elements to learn and enjoy – selecting the perfect pebbles, figuring out how to create elegant stacks, keeping your hand steady as you reach a tricky point and then gleefully knocking them down.**

YOU'LL NEED

★ Pebbles – hunt for the flattest stones in all sizes (or buy ethically sourced pebbles from a builders' merchants)
★ A steady hand

**1** Find a flat surface, such as a sandy spot, the top of a groyne or a large rock.

**2** Starting with the largest stone, balance them in a stack. Think carefully about how to place them, the size and weight of each. You don't need to work strictly large to small, as you might be able to place a larger stone on top of a small one. Consider whether the top of your stone will make a good base for the next stone.

**3** Work slowly and considerately, taking in your surroundings. Make your stack as tall or as beautiful as you can, then pause and take a photo of your creation.

**4** Knock down or dismantle your structure and put the stones back where you found them.

Try making sculptures that are more adventurous, such as a triple column base with flat rocks as planks across the columns.

## TIP

You know all those rules I laid down back on page 13? These apply to stone stacking too. In short, stay away from rock pools and rivers and don't disturb animal habitats, always put the stones back where you found them, don't touch anything historically important or sacred, don't give soil erosion a helping hand and respect the environment. The planet needs all the help it can get.

# RAINY DAYS

**Stuck inside? Bring cheer to grey afternoons with upbeat crafts, silly games and feel-good activities.**

# Garlands

**A colourful or cool garland lifts the spirits, brightens up a dark corner and brings cheer to a party. They can be tailored to seasons and occasions, customised with names and messages, or hung just to add a touch of fun. They look happy strung above children's beds, looped from mantlepieces or dangling in windows and you can make them from the most sumptuous card stock or humble newspapers. Sit and cut yours as a family, listening to music or chatting together. It's a great way to build excitement for an occasion.**

## YOU'LL NEED

★ Coloured card or paper
★ Scissors
★ Baker's twine, string or ribbon
★ PVA glue, hot glue gun or sticky tape

**Optional**
★ Round cookie cutter, small dish or glass
★ Compass and pencil

**Lots of Dots**

**1** Draw circles on your card or paper 3–10cm (1¼–4in) in diameter. Use a pencil and compass to sketch your rings or draw around cookie cutters, small dishes or glasses to create them if you find that easier.

**2** You'll need a pair of circles for each dot, but their colours don't have to match. If you can't be bothered to make two circles and don't mind seeing the twine glued to the back of your garland, then one for each dot will do.

**3** Cut out your circles.

**4** Using one from each pair, line up a row of circles. Think about how their sizes and colours flow together. Leave a gap of 2.5–5cm (1–2in) between each circle.

**5** Put a little bead of glue or loop of tape on the back of each circle, in the centre of the circle.

**6** Unspool your twine, and lay it along the line, circle by circle, onto each bead of glue or loop of tape. Leaving a generous end, cut your twine.

**7** Allow the garland to dry flat.

*continued*

**8** Put two more beads of glue on each circle and place the partner circles on top.

**9** Allow to dry, then string vertically or horizontally as the mood takes you.

Use this basic method to create colourful, tailor-made banners. You don't have to stick to circles; cut clouds, lightning bolts, triangles, stars or letters. Make chic monochrome garlands or use newspapers or magazines with a final coating of diluted PVA glue (see page 30) to keep them fresh. Try alternating small circles with large ones or cut additional small circles to stick centrally on the large circles.

YOU'LL NEED

★ Coloured paper, magazines, old wrapping paper, sheet music
★ Pencil and ruler
★ Sticky tape or glue
★ Scissors
★ String or ribbon
★ Plastic adhesive

**Flagging It Up**
To create the pennant-shaped garlands, adapt the previous instructions as follows.

**1** Choose your paper, then draw rectangles 5 x 15cm (2 x 6in), or use the template on page 173.

**2** Using scissors, cut out the shapes.

**3** Fold each rectangle in half and cut in a triangle where the two short ends meet.

**4** Fold each shape over the string or ribbon and secure in place with glue or sticky tape.

**5** Hang using plastic adhesive or tape.

# Tissue Paper Hair Dip Dye

It might sound crazy, but dyeing hair using tissue or crepe paper is easy and safe. Your new look will last for only two or three washes, which makes this activity perfect for school holiday fun. You might find tissue paper that's been used for packaging or you can buy both types of paper in craft shops. This works best on light-coloured hair, but still adds tones to dark locks; if you have brown or black hair, green paper works well. This activity can get messy, so don't do it near light-coloured carpets and wear old clothes. You'll need to lie down with your hair dipped in the bowl of dye so choose an area with enough space and a floor that cannot be damaged.

**1** Rip the tissue or crepe paper into strips.

**2** Take as many bowls as you have colours and add warm water until they are two-thirds full. Dissolve 1 tablespoon of salt in each and add a single colour of strips to each bowl.

**3** Section your hair into bunches, and secure with rubber bands.

**4** Place the bowls on the floor and lie down next to them, trailing the ends of your hair into the bowls. You'll have to stay like this for half an hour, so turn on the radio or put on some tunes beforehand.

**5** After half an hour, get up, taking care not to let your hair drip colour anywhere (you may want to wrap an old towel around your shoulders).

**6** Rinse your hair with cold water and dry as normal.

If you have short hair, can't be bothered to lie down for half an hour, want to colour more than just the ends or add highlights, take the soaked paper from the bowls and fasten it into your hair using rubber bands.

Be careful in the rain! If you are wearing light clothes and your hair gets wet, the colour may transfer.

YOU'LL NEED

★ Tissue or crepe paper in one or more colours
★ Bowls
★ Warm water
★ Salt
★ Rubber bands
★ An old towel

# Nature Collages

There's nothing more beautiful than nature, so bring its colours, curves and textures to your art. These temporary masterpieces use materials gathered from the wild to bring a flat template to life. Keep a jar of varied stones at hand and laminate your templates for a quick, five-minute activity to keep hands occupied in the time between supper and toothbrushing.

## YOU'LL NEED

★ Paper
★ Pens
★ Stones and pebbles of different sizes (flatter ones work well)

**Optional**
★ Other natural materials – leaves, petals, grass, twigs
★ Laminator
★ Washable felt-tip pens
★ PVA glue

**1** First make your templates. The idea is to spark imagination, so you might draw blank faces, bird outlines, monster and animal heads and legs, a tree trunk with branches, a rainbow. Or scenes: cityscapes, a lunar landscape or an undersea vista.

**2** If you want to reuse your templates, laminate them using eco-friendly laminate pouches or varnish using decoupage glue mix (see page 30).

**3** Bring out your stones and pebbles. Really young children might need supervision around small stones.

**4** Lay the stones on the sheets to create characters and faces, and to fill in all the missing parts of the pictures. Create stone monsters, aliens, animals and wild hairstyles. If you like, you can draw more detail on the stones using washable felt-tip pens.

**5** If you have access to a garden or park, head out to gather some extra bits and pieces to use. Leaves, pine cones, ferns, twigs, petals and grasses all work well and create more flowing, frond-filled and colourful lines.

# Sensory Boxes

**AGE: 3-6**

**We learn through touching and feeling. Activities that stimulate young children's senses are vital for their development. Not all of us are lucky enough to live near a beach or countryside, so bring the natural world into your garden, onto your balcony or into your living room with rock and paper-based sensory play.**

These basic toys can be played with in many ways. Remember that small children in close proximity to smaller rocks need constant close supervision.

Load up a shallow box or tray with...

### Gravel
Not only is this satisfying to run your hands through, but it's great to play with. Get your toy cars, diggers and bulldozers out and use them to move the gravel and rocks around.

### Bigger Pebbles
Wash the rocks, making sure none have jagged edges. Dig your hands into the rocks. What can you feel? Look at the shapes and colours and sort them accordingly. Talk about the sizes and textures and use them to practise counting. Pour in water and watch as it covers the rocks and changes their colour. Swish them around in the water.

### Shredded Paper
Use shredded paper from packing or create your own. Make thin paper strips using a shredder or – if you're patient – scissors. Hide objects for your toddler to find or just let them trail their fingers through the scrunchy paper...

What noise does it make? How does it look as you lift it and let it fall back into the box? The dream, of course, is to have enough shredded paper to fill a paddling pool.

### Paper Squidging
Tear up some toilet paper into big strips. Enjoy it as it is, or add water for a satisfyingly squidgy experience. Perhaps you might turn it into snowy mountains or squeeze it into balls. Newspaper, tissue paper and old wrapping paper also work well for paper squidging.

### Rock Soup
Fill a small bucket or bowl with water and add a few rocks. Are they vegetables? Dumplings? Can you use a ladle to serve your soup? Or are you a witch creating a terrible spell in her cauldron, adding newts' eyes and frogs' bones to your pot?

### Bean Bags
Use gravel or very small pebbles to fill simple bean bags. You want these to be extra safe, so make an inner bag from cotton fabric, completely sewn around, and enclose this in an outer, prettier bag. Use your bean bags for juggling, balancing on your heads, throwing to each other or just sitting on your shoulder like a pet parrot.

AGE: 7+

# Step Through a Piece of Paper

This trick is as much about the warm-up and hype as the illusion itself. You have to sell the idea to your audience, even if it's just your gran watching. Be boastful! 'Roll up! Roll up! See the incredible feat of being able to step through this tiny piece of paper!' Or challenge your audience. 'Who would like to bet that I won't be able to walk through this postcard?' Make a performance of it, but make sure you've practised well beforehand, so you can live up to your boast and not get laughed out of the living room.

YOU'LL NEED

★ Sheet of paper. Start practising with a piece approximately 21 x 30cm (8¼ x 12in, or A4 size), then move smaller and smaller as you get more confident. You should end up being able to step through a postcard-sized piece.
★ Scissors

**1** Fold your paper in half lengthways (see the step-by-step photos on the following pages).

**2** Cut into the folded edge 1cm (½in) from the end and make a slit; keep cutting until you're about 1.5cm (⅝in) from the other side of the paper.

**3** Repeat this at 2cm (¾in) intervals down the folded paper (you may need to adjust these measurements if you're using a postcard-sized piece of paper).

**4** Flip the paper over, and cut another series of slits from the other side, in between the ones you've already snipped. Again, stop the cuts 1.5cm (⅝in) from the other side of the paper.

**5** Leaving the two end loops intact, cut down the folded edge.

**6** Gently fold out your hoop.

**7** Step through the hoop smugly and receive your applause.

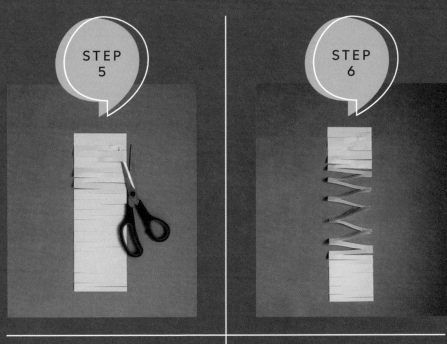

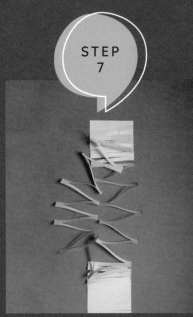

# Picture Consequences

A true cross-generational game, Picture Consequences or Exquisite Corpse, as it is sometimes known, is cast-iron guaranteed fun. Even small children can join the collaborative, draw-a-monster craziness – if you can sketch a head and feet, you're in! The aim is to create the silliest monster you can. The catch? You don't get to see the rest of the beast before you draw the next part.

## YOU'LL NEED

★ Sheet of paper for each player, approximately 21 x 30cm (8¼ x 12in, or A4 size)
★ Pen for each player
★ Hard surface for each player to draw on

**1** Give one sheet of paper and a pen to each player. Every player draws a head. It might be an animal face or human, or something really far out, such as an alien or a monster.

**2** Extend the two final neck lines a little, then fold back the paper to hide the face, leaving only the two neck lines visible.

**3** Each player passes their sheet of paper to the player on their left. No peeping!

**4** Now, using the two neck lines as a guide, draw a crazy body and arms. Extend the waist lines down and fold back the paper to hide the drawing. Pass all the drawings to the left again.

**5** Now draw two (or more) legs down to the lower leg. Extend the four lines of the ankles and fold again. Pass on the papers.

**6** Draw some freaky feet. Pass on your papers one last time.

**7** Take it in turns to open your sheets of paper. What kind of far-out creatures have you all produced?

## FUN FACT

Exquisite Corpse is said to have been invented in 1925 by surrealist artists André Breton, Yves Tanguy, Jacques Prévert and Marcel Duchamp, and it was a favourite game of Frida Kahlo!

# Melted Crayon Rocks

Art can be as much about the fun of making as the result. The feeling of half-drawing with/half-destroying crayons as they melt onto hot rocks is satisfying. The abstract, colour-bursting results are a blissful bonus. Go all-out rainbow for maximum fun or stay stylish with a restricted, muted palette. This craft is best kept for older children, as it involves hot rocks.

**YOU'LL NEED**

★ Largish flat rocks
★ Towel, for drying rocks and protecting your work surace
★ Old crayons
★ Oven (or a very, very warm day)
★ Baking tray
★ Kitchen foil or baking parchment
★ Oven mitts or tongs

**Optional**
★ Hairdryer
★ Potato peeler
★ PVA glue

**1** Wash and dry your rocks. Make sure they are bone dry, because wet pebbles and ovens aren't a good combination.

**2** Heat your oven to 170°C/fan 150°C/350°F/gas 4.

**3** While your oven is warming up, take the paper labels off the crayons. Discard any that are too short to avoid burned fingers.

**4** When the oven is ready, put the rocks on a baking tray and pop them in the oven. Let them heat up for 10–15 minutes. If it's a very warm day, you might be able to heat the rocks in the sun.

**5** Put a towel on your work surface and baking parchment or foil on top of that.

**6** Using oven mitts or tongs, remove one rock from the oven at a time. Be really, really careful! Those rocks are hot! Keep your fingers well away and only let the crayons touch the rocks.

**7** Carefully draw on the rock using the crayons. The wax will melt gently on to the surface. Let it pool in any holes or indentations. Layer colours on top of each other. Leave little pieces on top of the stones to melt.

**8** Let the rocks cool – this might take a couple of hours.

If you'd prefer to avoid the oven method and it's a cool day, heat your rocks with a hairdryer set on high pointed towards them while the artist draws on them with the wax crayons. Or use a potato peeler to scrape wax shavings from your crayons, sprinkle them on your rocks and melt them with a hairdryer. Use the recipe on page 30 to make decoupage glue and use it to seal your rocks.

**AGE: 6+**

# Paper Ladders and Trees

Create huge, seemingly never-ending ladders and plants out of a few sheets of boring old newspaper. These are such impressive tricks to have up your sleeve. Start by practising with a small piece of paper, then move up to a large newspaper-sized set of steps or beanstalk-sized tree. You'll be making ladders and plants that reach the ceiling in no time at all.

YOU'LL NEED

★ Newspapers
★ Sticky tape
★ Scissors

**Paper Ladder**

**1** Tape sheets of newspaper together to make a long strip. Depending on the shape and size of your paper, two or three sheets should be fine, but add in more if you want a bigger ladder. If you don't have tape, just roll each piece into the next (see the step-by-step photos on the following pages).

**2** Roll your newspaper strip up fairly tightly, using the short side as your starting point.

**3** A third in from the left edge, make a cut through the roll, cutting around two-thirds through the diameter.

**4** Do the same on the right edge.

**5** Bend both sides down at the cuts to form a bridge shape.

**6** Cut along the top of the middle section.

**7** Fold out the middle section and trim both sides, using the corners of the bridge as a starting point.

**8** Gently tease out the ladder, pulling up the rungs and the sides.

**9** Experiment with adding sheets of paper to the roll to make more rungs, or find out what happens when you roll it looser or tighter.

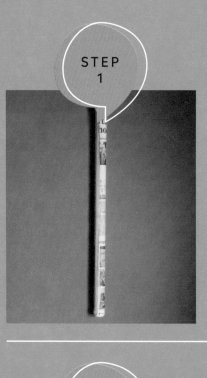

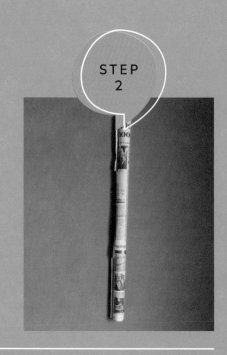

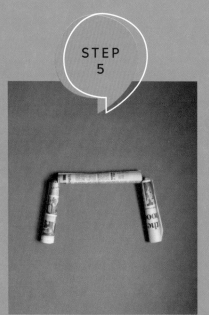

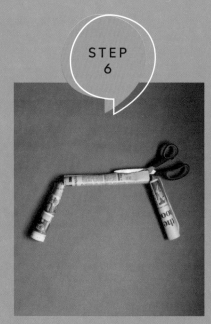

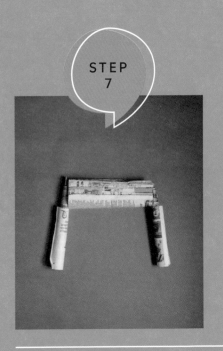

# FUN FACT

Paper ladders and trees make great centrepieces for a paper-tearing act. Why not practise and put on a show for your friends and family? Paper-tearing acts were popular during the Victorian era and in the first half of the 20th century. You could watch an artiste on stage at a rowdy music hall, creating giant paper lace doilies emblazoned with mottos and little pictures, folding elaborate paper ships or sending giant ladders soaring upwards into the top reaches of the auditorium. Perhaps you might revive that tradition?

**Paper Tree**

**1** Tape sheets of newspaper together to make a long strip. Depending on the shape and size of your paper, four or five pages should be fine.

**2** If you don't have tape, just roll each piece into the next.

**3** Start to roll the paper from the shortest side. Begin with a roll about 3cm (1¼in) in diameter, then roll up the rest fairly tightly, like a roll of wrapping paper on a tube.

**4** When you've rolled to the end, put a little tape across the end of the roll about a quarter of the way up the tube to hold. If you don't have tape, hold it in place.

**5** Take your scissors and make three or four even snips vertically from the top to about two-thirds down the tube. Depending on how much paper you've used, this might be fairly tough, so you may need help.

**6** Pull down the sections you've snipped so they hang down the outside of the newspaper tube.

**7** Gently tease up the tree from the centre. How high can you make it grow?

# Pebble Football

**Be warned – this game is addictive, thrilling and absorbing. And it can be played with the bare minimum of equipment. All you need are a few stones and a flat table. It's perfect to fill in time between lessons at school, on a rainy day or even on a train. Stone football is a variant of coin football, a pastime so popular there's even a video game version!**

## YOU'LL NEED

★ At least 3 small, similarly sized stones – flattish ones will work better than anything too round
★ Good-sized smooth table or flat surface
★ 2 players

**1** The aim of the game is the same as in football (soccer) – to score goals.

**2** The players stand on opposite sides of the table.

**3** One player forms a 'goal' using one hand, forefinger and little finger extended on the edge of the table, or by using stones to mark posts.

**4** The other player throws three stones on to the table. They then progress towards the goal by pushing, tapping or flicking the stone at the back of the group through the gap formed by the other two.

**5** When they get to the stage that it's impossible to get the back stone through the others and play can no longer progress, their turn is over, so they pick up the stones and give them to the other player for their go.

**6** Players score by shooting one of their stones through the fingertip goal.

The game is endlessly adaptable. You might add another stone as a goalkeeper or have a specific method of shooting at the goal. If one of the stones is flicked off the table, you might make 'throw in' rules.

**AGE: 2+**

ADULT
SUPERVISION IS
RECOMMENDED

# Paper and Stone Instruments

**Get ready to rock and roll (up some paper)! Rustle up some home-made musical instruments and form a band. Here are three ideas – flute, shaker and lithophone – to get you started.**

**YOU'LL NEED**

**Paper Flute**
★ Sheet of strong, thick paper, approximately 21 x 30cm (8¼ x 12in, or A4 size)
★ Sticky tape or rubber bands
★ Scissors

### Paper Flute
This will need adult supervision, as you need sharp scissors and it can be fiddly.

**1** Roll the sheet of paper into a 4cm (1½in) diameter tube and tape down the entire length of the seam or secure the tube with a rubber band.

**2** Cut two 2cm (¾in) slits horizontally in the tube, about 5cm (2in) down from the top. The hole should be opposite the seam of the tube. Cut out the sides of the slits to form a square hole.

**3** Poke your scissors down from the top of the tube, between the outside layer and the other layers of paper. Use your scissors or finger to separate the top from the other layers, and push them into a V shape.

**4** Blow down the flute between the layers. A note should sound! If it doesn't, then keep poking and fiddling until you get a sound. You may need to make the hole bigger to make it work.

**5** Make finger holes in your flute – cut them as you did in step 2, but make the holes a bit smaller so you can cover them with your fingers when you play the flute. Experiment to find out how they affect the tone and pitch of each note.

## Shaker

★ Clean plastic bottle with a lid
★ Things to decorate your bottle – ribbons, stickers, washi tape, marker pens or tissue paper and glue
★ Very small pebbles or gravel

## Lithophone

★ 7 sticks or pieces of driftwood
★ String
★ Scissors
★ Thin, flat stones of very different lengths (slate works beautifully)
★ Something metal to bang them – a small hammer or a spanner will do

## Shaker

Small children should always be supervised when around small stones, even if they're in a bottle with a cap!

**1** Decorate your bottle using paper, ribbons, washi tape and pens. Cut up strips of tissue paper to make tassels that move with your shaker.

**2** Put your small pebbles or gravel into the bottom of your bottle. You don't need many; just enough to cover the bottom.

**3** Screw the bottle cap on tightly.

**4** Shake!

## Lithophone

Musical instruments made out of rocks that are struck to produce notes are called lithophones and are found across the world. They can be as simple as a rock formation that chimes when it's hit with a stick or as gorgeously complex as the 'steinspiel' required by composer Carl Orff. Icelandic band, Sigur Rós constructed a slate marimba using rocks found in their native land. Why not try making your own?

**1** First form a frame. It's easiest to make a goalpost-shaped construction. Use six of your sticks to make two tripods (three-legged stands), secured with string. Balance the third stick across the two tripods. Alternatively, create a frame using whatever you have around – a pipe tied to the backs of two chairs, a laundry dryer frame, or simply use an existing bar.

**2** Tie string around your rocks and suspend them from the third stick. If you have the tools, drilling through stones to make a hole in them will make your lithophone even more tuneful.

**3** Experiment with different shapes, types and thicknesses of stones and find out what noises they make.

# Party Games

**Need some quick-fire, crowd-pleasing activities for a party? These two favourites are tried and tested, take only seconds to prepare and are guaranteed to get everyone laughing.**

**YOU'LL NEED**

★ Toilet rolls
★ Source of music

**Mummy Mayhem**

Warning: this Ancient Egyptian-themed game always ends in total chaos! Play it in a large space or move anything breakable out of harm's way.

**1** Divide your guests into pairs. Give each pair a toilet roll.

**2** The aim of the game is to wrap your partner from head to toe in toilet roll.

**3** When the music starts, so does the game. Give the players a count down, then go! Choose a suitably crazed song to ramp up the energy levels.

**4** At the end of the song – or after three minutes – everyone must put down their rolls and step away from their mummy partners.

**5** Put on another song. The mummies start to dance.

**6** A judge decides who's made the best mummy and that pair are declared the winners.

**7** Tear off your toilet roll, swap roles and play another round.

Be sure to save the post-mummy toilet roll after you've finished. Either put it into the recycling bin or use it for another project, perhaps Sensory Play (see page 111).

★ A big stack of
newspapers
★ Sticky tape
★ Scissors
★ Stopwatch
or phone

**Optional**
★ Felt-tip pens
★ Ribbon
★ Feathers
★ Toilet roll

**Newspaper Catwalk**

Flex those fashion muscles and create clothing designs from paper. This game works best for older children, teens and adults, or mixed-age teams.

**1** Split your guests into teams; four on each is a good number. You'll also need a judge.

**2** Each team selects a model.

**3** The aim of the game is to design and make a head-to-toe outfit using just the materials provided.

**4** Set the timer for 10–15 minutes. And go! Think paper dresses, cone-shaped hats, capes or basic shoes. Try shredding paper to add texture. Perhaps you might create a wig or make something truly avant-garde and weird. If you have extra decorations, incorporate them wisely.

**5** When the time is up, all teams must put their materials down and step away from the models.

**6** The models take to the 'catwalk' and strut up and down the room, while the judge decides who has done the best job.

Recycle the paper or use it for a papier-mâché project (see pages 36–41).

# Magazine Collages

AGE: 3+

The word 'collage' was first used by European artists Georges Braque and Pablo Picasso at the beginning of the 20th century, but the technique of finding different bits and bobs and pasting them into a new piece of art has been around for thousands of years – since the invention of paper in China around 200 BC. The technique became a craze in the 19th century, when Victorians – mainly women – started to glue newly invented photographs into books, accompanied by cut-out words and pictures. The technique was embraced in the 20th century as artists created art that made a statement through clever or silly contrasts.

Your collages can be as simple or as complex as you wish. It's a satisfying, meditative process; sitting at a table, leafing through magazines and newspapers and pretty bits of paper, then cutting and gluing them. And it can be really, really funny. A rainy afternoon will pass by in a whirl of scissors, laughter and sticky fingers.

YOU'LL NEED

★ PVA glue
★ Brushes or spreaders
★ Scissors
★ Paper

**1** Leaf through your stack of papers (see suggestions on page 134), and select images and text that leap out. Snip out any pictures and words or sentences that appeal to you. They don't have to be dramatic or funny on their own; it's all about contrasting them with other pieces. Think about how you cut around them; it's often most effective to select part of a picture – a person's head, a speech bubble, some silly shoes, a tree.

**2** Keep finding and snipping treasures until you have a small stack of pieces.

**3** Take your sheet of paper and arrange your cut-outs on it. Move them around and play with them. This is the fun part!

*continued*

**A pick 'n' mix selection of:**
★ Newspapers
★ Magazines
★ Wrapping paper
★ Greetings cards
★ Comics
★ Tickets
★ Old photos
  (check first
  that they're not
  treasured ones
  or make and use
  photocopies)
★ Old postcards

**Optional**
★ Watered-down
  PVA glue
  (3 parts glue to
  1 part water)
★ Ribbons
★ Felt-tip pens or
  metallic pens
★ Googly eyes
★ Stickers
★ Eco-glitter

You might create something weird – a seal's head on a man's body, with a speech bubble saying 'WOT?!', a roller-skating elephant or an alien watching TV. The surrealist art movement was very fond of making collages as it appealed to their mischievous, playful nature; let your imagination run riot.

Perhaps you'll choose to create something more thoughtful or even political – fashion images contrasted with serious news headlines or politicians with thought bubbles over their heads revealing their real plans. Collages can also be simple and beautiful, contrasting patterns, a mass of flowers and kittens, or even plans and ideas for your bedroom makeover.

Younger children might prefer to keep things more simple. Use a food magazine to cut out vegetables and fruit and create a greengrocer's store front, or make a beach scene.

**4** Add ribbons, eco-glitter, googly eyes or your own squiggles and writing if you wish.

**5** Happy with your artwork? Glue down the pieces.

**6** Want to varnish it and keep your pieces in place? Gently brush watered-down PVA glue over the surface and leave to dry.

## TIP

Keep a collage box. Every time you see a picture, phrase or typeface that appeals to you, cut it out and pop it in your box. Keep old greetings cards and fragments of wrapping paper in there, ready to take out at the first hint of a drizzly Sunday afternoon. If your pictures, books, postcards, tickets or treasures are too valuable to cut up, make photocopies to use instead.

# Ice and Stone Votive

Light up cold wintry nights with these glistening, glowing lamps. Ice showcases the natural beauty of stones, lending them a natural shine. This is a magical winter activity for all festivities, while the end result is chic enough to pass muster even at a teenage party.

## YOU'LL NEED

★ Water
★ 2 plastic pots or tin cans, one bigger than the other
★ Sticky tape
★ Scissors
★ 7-10 small, pretty stones
★ A cold night or a freezer
★ A battery-powered or real tea light

**Optional**

★ Natural materials such as ferns, berries, leaves or flower petals
★ Food colouring

**1** Pour 2-3cm (¾-1¼in) of water into the bigger pot.

**2** Float the smaller pot in the water. Keeping it as centred as you can, use four strips of tape to secure it to the bigger pot.

**3** Put your stones into the gap between the pots, spreading them out evenly. Don't use too many!

**4** If you wish to add natural materials, push them into the gaps between the pots. Again, less is more! For coloured ice, add a few drops of food colouring.

**5** Fill the gap between the two pots with water. If the smaller pot rises too much, use some bigger stones to help weigh it down and keep it in place. The idea is to have an even band of water beneath and around the sides of the smaller pot.

**6** Carefully place the whole thing upright into your freezer or, if it's cold enough, outside. Leave overnight.

**7** Rinse a little hot water around the inside and outside of the lantern, and turn it out.

**8** Pop a tea light into your lantern. Twinkly!

If you'd like to have stones all the way up your lantern, freeze it in stages, adding stones to each layer. If you want a clearer freeze, use distilled water boiled twice instead of water straight from the tap (faucet). You might even try putting your lantern into an insulated container with the lid off before freezing. This will force your lantern to chill more slowly from the top down, which helps keep the ice transparent.

# Boxes

**This game of skill only needs a scrap of paper and a pen. Play it any time you need to while away a few minutes; keep a notepad and a few pens at hand for instant matches in waiting rooms, on trains or when waiting in the car. Suitable for two to four players.**

## YOU'LL NEED

★ Piece of paper
★ Pen

**Optional**
★ Graph or squared paper

**1** Mark out a rectangular grid of dots on your piece of paper. This is easier if you're using graph or squared paper. Your grid can be any size, but a 12 x 12 or 15 x 15 board works really well.

**2** The first player takes the pen and joins two adjacent dots horizontally or vertically. This is a move. They pass on the pen.

**3** The second player does the same.

**4** When a player completes all four sides of a box, they mark it with their initial. They then take another turn. Their turn continues until they cannot form any more boxes. They make one more line and then pass the paper on to the next player.

**5** The winner is the player who, when all the boxes are claimed, has the most marked with their initial.

The game may sound simple and the rules are, indeed, straightforward. However, once players become familiar with the gameplay, tactics become important. If your strategy works, you should form 'alleyways' of boxes and force your opponent to open up more pathways to you. Sometimes you may need to sacrifice boxes early on in order to form more lucrative strips later in the match. It's addictive, fierce stuff, not for the faint-hearted.

# Fortune Teller

**What lies in your future? Will you be rich? Famous? Get a big old boil on the end of your nose? Find out what is in store for you and your friends with this classic fortune teller.**

YOU'LL NEED

★ Square piece of paper
★ Scissors
★ Pens or pencils

**1** If your paper isn't already square, cut it into one.

**2** Fold your paper in half diagonally both ways and make a crease (see the step-by-step photos on the following pages). Open it.

**3** Fold your paper in half horizontally and make a crease. Open it again.

**4** Fold each corner into the centre.

**5** Turn it over. Fold each corner into the centre.

**6** Fold the square in half lengthways.

**7** Poke two fingers and thumbs into each flap and wiggle them about a bit until the fortune teller opens freely both ways.

**8** Unfold it once into a little square again and lift one of the triangular flaps. Write a fortune – see page 143 for some inspiration. Repeat for each triangle until you've written eight fortunes.

**9** Fold the flaps back down and write numbers 5–12 on each triangle; eight in total.

**10** Turn your teller over and write numbers 1–4 on each of the square flaps.

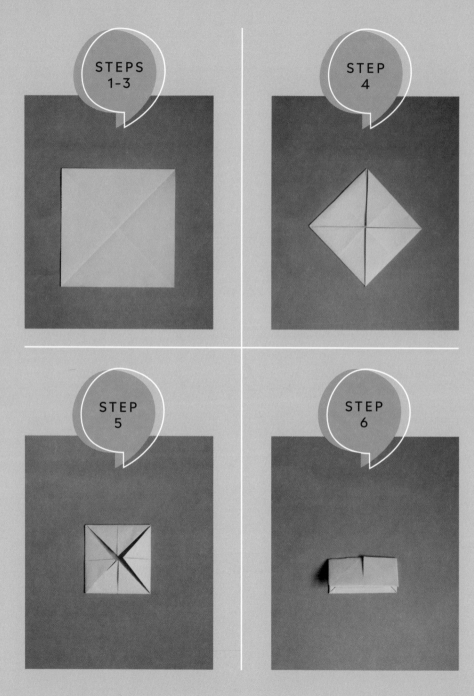

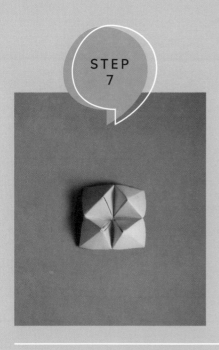

To play with your fortune teller, put your forefingers and thumbs in the flaps and offer it closed to whoever wishes to know their future. They should choose a number from the top. Using your fingers and thumbs, open and close your teller horizontally and vertically that number of times. Your victim then chooses a number from inside the teller, and you do the same opening and closing. Repeat this four times. The number chosen on the final turn is the fortune; open the flap and read what's beneath!

# FORTUNE-SPIRATION

Ideas to write beneath the flaps:
★ You will meet an important person while dancing
★ Keep smiling!
★ Your happiest days will be by the sea
★ Keep trying to eat cabbage. You'll get there!
★ Avoid dark clouds, as lightning can strike at any moment
★ What's that smell?

# Paper Pom-Poms

**Fill your house with these deceptively easy-to-make, multi-coloured balls of wonder. More eco-friendly than balloons, they'll last until they get too dusty to bear. Keep to a single colour or layer contrasting combinations – citrus brights for summer parties, oranges for Halloween or rich metallics, reds and greens for Christmas. Vary the sizes for extra impact.**

## YOU'LL NEED

★ Tissue paper
★ Scissors
★ Wire or staple gun
★ String

**1** Take ten sheets of 50 x 70cm (19½ x 27½in) tissue paper, all one colour or two or three contrasting hues. Lay them neatly on top of each other. If you're using two or more colours, alternate the colours.

**2** Fold the whole stack concertina-style, each fold should be 3–6cm (1¼–2½in) wide. Keep going until you've folded the whole stack of tissue paper.

**3** You'll now have a long, thin shape. Using your scissors, trim off the ends of that shape into a curve.

**4** Fold the whole concertina in half to find the centre. Wrap wire around or staple this centre point.

**5** Carefully pull the layers apart, keeping your pom-pom even and symmetrical.

**6** Tie string to your wire or around the centre and use to hang your pom-pom.

**7** Make more!

## TIP

For an ombré (shaded) effect, start your stack with a dark colour, then layer lighter and lighter shades of that colour through to white.

# IMAGINATION AND FOLKLORE

**The basic nature of stones, paper and scissors means they have a rich history, magic and myth to explore. Use these elements as a springboard for your own imagination.**

# Pet Rock

**If a dog is too demanding, a cat requires too much responsibility and you're not keen on rabbits, why not keep a pet rock? A rock takes up very little room, you don't need to toilet train it and it can go without food for long periods. You can devote as much or as little time as you wish to your little friend.**

YOU'LL NEED

★ Smooth stone

**Optional**
★ Googly eyes
★ Glue
★ Paint

First, find your stone. What are you looking for in your rock? A friend you can carry in your pocket? Something bigger that might sit on your window sill? Or a pal who'll sit in your garden or on your balcony, patiently waiting for you in all weathers?

Decide if you've got a little lady or tiny man. Or perhaps your stone is more of an it? Give your new sidekick a name, perhaps inspired by their colour, shape or where you found them.

Give your friend a bath. You might like to stick on googly eyes, paint a face or leave them as an featureless enigma.

Make them a cosy bed. Rocks might look hard, but they like to sleep soft. Line a little box with cotton wool or use an old silk scarf. On cold nights they might like to snuggle in your bed.

Rocks aren't big eaters, but yours might like to be rubbed with sweet-smelling petals and herbs. Try mint leaves, orange blossom or rosemary needles and see how your pet responds.

Take your rock on days out. They love to hang out with their friends on the beach – make sure yours doesn't get lost – or to go on long walks with their favourite buddy – you! Keep yours in your pocket or make a soft bag that will hang off a belt.

Rocks are the only pets you can really take to school. Slip yours in your bag – he'll be there to reassure you when he's needed; give him a quick pat if you're stressed or frustrated. When you return home, your pebbly fellow might like to hop out of your school bag and sit and watch as you do your homework.

Above all, give your stone some love and he'll be a reliable, steadfast friend, always there for you.

# Selfie Accessories

**AGE: 4+**

Pouty, serious pictures are out. Silly, funny selfies are in! Jazz up your photo portraits with these colourful, easy-to-make accessories that are picture perfect for parties, play days with friends or just to cheer you up on a boring day.

**YOU'LL NEED**

★ Plain card or thick paper
★ Marker pens or thick felt-tip pens
★ Scissors
★ Dowelling, garden sticks or small bamboo canes
★ Sticky tape or glue

**Optional**
★ Glitter card
★ Coloured cellophane (or old sweet/candy wrappers)
★ Eco-glitter
★ Ribbons
★ Washi tape
★ Metallic card or paper

**1** Using marker pens or felt-tip pens, draw out your chosen accessory on your card or thick paper. Use our pictures opposite and on page 9 for inspiration. Make your pieces big, bold and use thick lines to draw them. Try moustaches, lips and teeth, hats, hair, glasses and speech bubbles.

**2** Cut them out, leaving the thick lines on the pieces (a thick outline adds definition and makes them look neater).

**3** Use marker pens or felt-tip pens to colour each accessory in bright colours. Add extra embellishments – cut out little 'wings' from glitter card or paper for your glasses and add colourful lenses by sticking cellophane to the back of the frames. Frost lips with red eco-glitter.

**4** Attach the dowelling or stick to each accessory using tape or glue. Some designs work best on a stick set centrally, for others such as glasses secure at one side. If using glue, allow it to dry.

**5** If you wish, decorate your sticks with ribbon or washi tape.

**6** Hold up your accessories to your face and strike a pose!

## TIP

Organising a wedding or big party? Make a stack of these and leave them on guests' tables. They'll give the night's snaps a focus and create a uniform look to everyone's photographs. Clever, huh?

# Cobble Cacti

**AGE: 5+**

Spiky, exotic and dramatic, real-life cacti are not only on trend but easy to look after. However, if you don't even want the minimal hassle of watering, make a pot or two of these luscious desert dwellers. Can you believe these cartoon-like succulents are made from stones? They look bright along a windowsill or varnish them and create a mini garden on a balcony.

## YOU'LL NEED

★ Flat, suitably shaped stones
★ Acrylic paint in white, greens, yellows, oranges and reds
★ Brushes
★ Acrylic paint pens in white and black
★ Small flower pots
★ Gravel or sand

### Optional
★ White primer spray
★ Fimo (or polymer) clay in red or pink
★ Varnish

**1** Select flat stones that are long and thin or teardrop-shaped. Wash and dry them.

**2** Spray them with primer paint or paint them with a base coat of white acrylic paint. Leave to dry.

**3** Choose a colour for your cactus. Greens work well, but contrast your emeralds with yellows, reds and even oranges. Paint your main colour and leave to dry. You may like to add contrasting stripes to some; dark and light green work well.

**4** Using white or black acrylic paint pens or a thin brush, trace patterns onto your plants. Try rows of dots, vertical lines studded with circles or arrows, and little three-pronged shapes. Look at the photo opposite for inspiration.

**5** If you wish, at the top add little red or pink flowers using paint or Fimo clay.

**6** If the cacti are going outside, varnish them and leave to dry.

**7** Plant your cacti in pots filled with gravel. Group them in twos or threes or leave larger plants solo.

# Make-A-Face Kit

This is a fun-to-make, funnier-to-play game that you can build up slowly by creating more stones when you have a few minutes to spare. Each stone has a painted or decoupaged feature, perfect for arranging into crazy faces. They're easy to make, so if you have a large family, the older children might like to paint or decoupage them for their younger brothers and sisters. Pull your set out when you have a few minutes to fill and see who can construct the silliest face.

YOU'LL NEED

★ Flat pebbles of different sizes
★ Acrylic paints
★ Brushes

OR

★ Magazines and newspapers
★ Scissors
★ PVA glue

**Optional**
★ Varnish
★ Storage bag

**1** Wash and dry your pebbles.

**2** Sort them into different shapes. Long pebbles make good noses and mouths. Little round ones suit beady eyes. Use different sizes to mix things up – the aim is to go as crazy as you can.

**3** Paint or cut out appropriate pictures from magazines and decoupage (see page 30) funny features onto your stones. Make eyes, noses, mouths, ears, even hair and hats.

**4** Make sure the expressions are varied, so include sad and happy mouths, crying and winking eyes.

**5** Why not include different types of features? Try painting cat eyes, spiral irises, snake mouths, alien noses or bunny ears.

**6** Let your paint dry, then varnish if you wish.

**7** Play with your face stones by combining all the features into the funniest face you can make. Keep them safely in a soft bag.

# Henges

AGE: 3+

**Rocks can be sacred and meaningful. There are prehistoric stone structures across the globe, possibly once used for worship, as a calendar or for sacrifices. Look online at the iconic arches of Stonehenge in the UK, the target-shaped Rujm el-Hiri in Israel or the 3000-stone monument at Carnac in France.**

If you'd like to visit a real-life ancient stone structure, find a good online map or buy a guidebook and search for one near you. There's something magical about stroking a stone or ducking inside a chamber that's been in place for thousands of years. Imagine who else has run their fingers along the surface of these rocks, or try to figure out what the construction was originally used for (but most of the time no-one knows for sure). Be respectful; the stones meant a lot to people in the past and are still regarded by many as special today.

Why not make your own circle? Those lucky enough to have a large back garden might make a big, permanent monument. If you build yours at winter solstice (which, in the northern hemisphere falls between 21 and 22 December and in the southern hemisphere falls between 21 and 22 June) or summer solstice (which, in the northern hemisphere falls between 20 and 21 June and in the southern hemisphere falls between 21 and 22 December), then you can even align your stones with the rising sun. How exciting to have your own structure, which you can use for ceremonies, dancing or as a place to sit and think.

However, most of us won't have room for something on such a large scale. But that doesn't matter. Stone circles can be created anywhere – on the beach, in a meadow or in a park. How yours looks and what you use it for is entirely up to you. You choose the number of rocks, the shape and the size. You might plonk them down randomly, or feel their vibrations to work out where they should stand. The picture here shows one created using slate pieces 10–15cm (4–6in) high, which was reminiscent of Orkney's Standing Stones of Stenness. You could go a little larger scale and haul some bigger rocks around, or even downsize. Try creating a mini henge in a bowl of sand, or try making your own kit of tiny stones you can fit into a matchbox and construct wherever you happen to be for a moment of calm and contemplation.

**AGE: 4+**

# Magical Hag Stone Necklace

**Have you ever picked up a stone with a hole all the way through? Search on a pebbled beach long enough and you're sure to find one. Some people call them hag stones, others name them serpent's eggs or witch rocks, but there's one thing everyone agrees on: they have magical powers.**

## YOU'LL NEED

★ Small hag stone or stones
★ Leather cord or string (choose yours in red if you want to increase your chances of seeing supernatural creatures)

**Optional**
★ Beads or charms
★ Toddler-safe clasp
★ Paint
★ Brushes
★ Varnish

There are many stories about these pebbles: if you peer through the hole, you'll spot fairies, or a tiny door might open to another realm. Some tales tell how they help make spells, ward off witches and the dead, and keep livestock safe. People once believed that keeping one under your bed would help ease aches and pains. Others claimed that you might only leave a town if you found a hag stone on its beach. In Germany, they're known as adder stones, said to be formed from snake poison.

**1** Clean your hag stone. Paint and varnish it if you wish.

**2** Hold the ends of your length of cord or string and make a loop. Poke the end of your loop through the stone's hole. Push the two ends of the string through the loop and pull tight.

**3** Thread beads, more little hag stones or charms onto the two strings, so they sit above the main rock.

**4** Cut the end of the string to the length required and tie. If you're making the necklace for a young child, use a toddler-safe necklace clasp.

**5** Keep your stone close to ward off those evil spirits, or hold it up to your eye to spot fairies.

### How is a Hag Stone Formed?
The holes are formed in two ways. Smaller pebbles grind against the larger stone's surface, creating pits. Eventually, a stone will become stuck in the pit and wear away at the larger rock, creating a hole. Less commonly, the holes are burrowed as homes by a bivalve mollusc called the piddock.

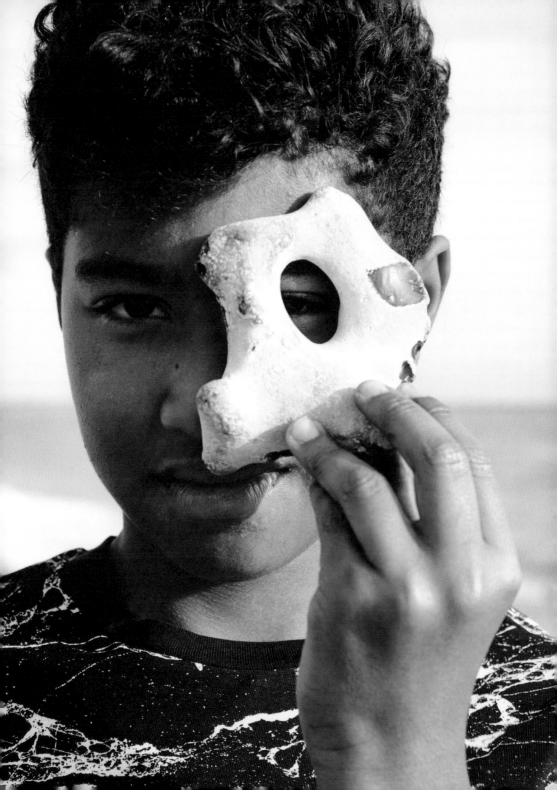

# Story Stones

**AGE: 3+**

**Not only are these little illustrated rocks fun and absorbing to make, they also fire your family's imagination. Telling tales from a standing start can be intimidating and tricky, but these home-made prompts will nurture and hone everyone's myth-spinning skills, from toddlers to teenagers.**

## YOU'LL NEED

★ 10–20 equally sized, flat stones, about 5cm (2in) wide
★ Soft pencil
★ Paints (thick, acrylics are best for painting stones) or marker pens

### Optional
★ Varnish or watered-down PVA glue (see page 30)
★ A small drawstring pouch or repurposed tote bag

Think about what kind of picture prompts will be appropriate for your family. You might be a crown-sword-castle kind of gang, or perhaps an alien-blaster-spaceship crew. You could make different bags to bring out according to your mood – a traditional fairy-tale set, a mythological set, a digital romance set or a jungle-themed set. Or make things more fun and mix up your worlds. Some children might need very definite objects to direct their thoughts, others might thrive on more abstract symbols. You need a healthy mix of characters, settings, story-drivers and resolutions. These categories are fluid, for example, a character such as a witch might also be a story driver. Some examples might include:

### Characters
★ Fairy
★ Unicorn
★ Fish
★ King
★ Queen
★ Dragon
★ Witch
★ Wolf
★ Prince
★ Princess

### Settings
★ Castle
★ Mountain
★ Sea
★ Tree
★ Snow

### Story drivers
★ Star
★ Wheel
★ Book
★ Pen
★ Ghost
★ Bow and arrow
★ Spaceship
★ Crown
★ Letter
★ Clock

### Resolutions
★ Heart
★ Magic wand
★ Key
★ Sword

*continued*

**1** Take your pencil and mark out your designs. Soft pencil should show up on even the darkest stones.

**2** Use your paints or pens to colour the stones. You could go minimal and keep things stylish in monochrome or break out the colours and create mini works of art. Perhaps you'll stick to one style of design – Japanese, runic or graphic shapes, or just paint in your own style.

**3** Let the stones dry, varnish them if you wish and keep them in a special bag or box.

There are subtly different ways to use the stones to create stories that you share together. Perhaps you'll pull out seven random designs each, take time to mull over them, then tell your story. Or maybe you'll pull one from a bag and let that direct a twisty-turny tale. You could separate the stones into piles according to their categories and take one from each group in turn; this helps a little with creating a more definite story structure.

## ALTERNATIVELY...

★ Cut pictures from magazines or old story books to fit, glue them onto the stones, then varnish using watered-down PVA glue (this is what I did for the photo).
★ Or paint the stones in blackboard paint and encourage your children to make their own designs in chalk.
★ Try something a little more abstract and emblazon your stones using designs that can be interpreted in different ways. For example, a zig-zag line might be mountains or teeth, a lightning bolt a weather phenomenon, an idea or a spell, and small dashes might be rain, time passing or the sea.

# Stone Skeletons

AGE: 3+

Chalk horses dot the hills of Britain, carved into the landscape by hands ancient and new. Put a deliciously horror-filled twist on this tradition and make a bone-rattling skeleton in the sand or on a hillside. This is a good project to do on a beach or landscape that's rich in chalk, but you can use white or light-coloured stones to equally good effect.

## YOU'LL NEED

★ Chalk or white stones
★ Sandy beach or grassy hillside

**1** You'll need lots of white or chalk stones in different sizes. Include some bigger ones for the head, long thin stones for the ribs and round flat stones for the hips.

**2** If you're on a beach, lightly sketch out a rough figure in the sand. If you want, use sand dug from elsewhere on the beach to build up a formation 5–10cm (2–4in) high on top of the lines you've sketched.

**3** If you're in the countryside, find a place – preferably on the side of a hill – with short grass. Somewhere grazed by sheep or near a rabbit warren might be perfect.

**4** Use your stash of chalk or white stones to form a skeleton. Use a big stone for the skull and two or three oval stones for teeth. Form the lines of bones using smaller stones. If you have long, thin rocks, use them for the ribs. If not, build them using little rocks. Use circular, flat stones for the hips and little thin stones for the toes.

**5** Stand back to admire your skeleton. Take a photo, then return your rocks to where you found them.

Don't fancy forming a skeleton? Try making a white horse, a giant or a symbol of something important to you or your family.

# Pebble Art Family

**Pebble pictures of your family warm the heart and are soothing to make together. The art to this craft is all in the stone-picking and arranging. You need small, flat stones of different shapes and sizes. Take your time piecing them together, you'll find the perfect fit, but it may take a while. As you're using a hot glue gun or strong glue, this activity will need adult supervision.**

## YOU'LL NEED

★ Plenty of small, flat stones
★ Driftwood
★ Card or thick paper
★ Strong glue or hot glue gun
★ Scissors

**Optional**
★ Deep or box frame
★ Pen or pencil
★ Seaweed
★ Sea glass
★ Twigs
★ Twine
★ Letter transfers or stickers

**1** Wash your stones and leave them to dry.

**2** If you're using a frame, cut your card or paper to fit.

**3** Sort through your stones and pieces of driftwood and think about how they'll work together. Each family member needs a stone to represent the head and one for their body. Adding an arm works well, too.

**4** Pick appropriate sizes and colours for each member of the family … and don't forget your pets!

**5** Arrange your pebbles on the card. This stage may take some time, but revel in that. Think of it like a jigsaw and be patient. This is a Zen craft.

**6** If you have a small piece of driftwood, use it as the 'base' for your figures or perhaps form a roof above the heads.

**7** Keep arranging. You might like to form balloons from a small pebble and a short length of twine, and draw on the knot with a pencil. Perhaps use sea glass, twigs and seaweed to form trees or waves.

**8** If you want to, ink or pencil a few words – the name of your family or a word or phrase that means something to you all. If your handwriting isn't very neat, use transfers or stickers.

**9** When you're happy with your picture, use strong glue or a hot glue gun to secure the pebbles to the card. Leave it to dry.

**10** Pop the card into the frame, or just leave it as it is.

# Brown Bag Masks

**AGE: 2+**

**Wearing a mask allows you to become someone (or something) else without needing a full costume. Will you choose to be a superhero, a monster, a mythical creature or something more sinister? You could make different masks to suit your moods!**

### YOU'LL NEED

★ Paper bags that will fit comfortably over the head of the wearer – try rectangular-based grocery bags or make your own from brown paper
★ Felt-tip pens
★ Scissors

**Optional**
★ String
★ Paint
★ Glue
★ Coloured and metallic paper
★ Scraps of cloth
★ Bottle caps
★ Wool
★ Feathers
★ Sticks
★ Leaves

**1** Snip any handles off the bag. Pop the bag on the head of the wearer-to-be and cut it to shape. You may need to trim the bottom off and cut V shapes to sit over the shoulders.

**2** Use a pen or pencil to mark where the eyes are. Take the bag off and cut out eyeholes.

**3** Now comes the fun part! Create a character and draw their face on the bag. Stick to black pen and abstract designs or go wild with multiple colours. Decorate with string, paint, coloured paper or scraps of cloth. Try adding string hair, flashy metallic paper eyelids and bright pink lips.

**4** If you have someone in the household who isn't keen on wearing masks, cut a hole in the front of a bag and draw around it; you might make their face the centre of a flower or have them as part of a classic painting.

**Safety Note**
We know you know this, but never, ever use a bag that's not made out of paper for this craft.

## TIP

Why not get all the members of your household to create their own mask to represent themselves and take weird family portraits? Or use your characters as the basis for a play; make scenery and props out of cardboard for a coherent look.

## WHAT WILL YOU CHOOSE TO BE?

★ Bird
★ Superhero
★ Monster
★ Animal
★ Mythical creature
★ Robot
★ Alien
★ Zombie
★ Old person
★ Baby
★ Yourself, but scarier!

# Dowse to Find Treasure, Water or Your Future

Imagine being able to find underground streams, buried treasure, something you've lost or even see into your future, purely by using a stone and some thread. Although controlled scientific tests tell us that dowsing cannot work, the ancient art of using a pendulum to find stuff is fun to try out.

### YOU'LL NEED

★ Small stone with a hole in it (see page 158)
★ Cotton thread, dental floss, thin leather cord or chain

**Optional**
★ Large-scale map or hand-drawn map

**1** Poke your thread through the hole in your stone and tie it tight. Cut the thread to about 25cm (10in), although you may need to experiment to find what length is right for you. This is your pendulum. It should be long enough to swing gently with only a little movement from your hand, but not so long that it's unwieldy, heavy or likely to get tangled easily.

**2** Hold your pendulum at the top of your thread.

**3** Now find how your pendulum responds to you. Gently give the pendulum a little movement, then ask it to give you a response to a question that requires the answer 'yes'. Give the pendulum some time to settle. According to dowsing theory, at this point it will demonstrate a positive movement; perhaps it will spin, maybe it will move in a circle or back and forth. This is your 'yes' indicator.

**4** Decide what you'd like to search for and visualise it. You might want to discover an underground stream, buried treasure, something you've lost in your house or a long-lost archaeological site. Head to a park, field or a chosen room in your home.

**5** Walk around holding the pendulum, letting it swing. Dowsers believe that the pendulum will use its 'yes' indicator to tell you when you are standing over buried treasure, a stream or even an electricity cable.

**6** Why not test it out? Bury some 'treasure' and see if a dowser can find it.

**7** If it's windy outside, your pendulum will be disturbed, so try map dowsing instead. Hold your pendulum above a map and let it tell you, via its 'yes' indicator, where to find treasure, water or electricity.

## TIP

Some people believe that pendulums can answer questions that have been troubling you or that they can tell you about the future. Why not try out this mystical activity? Simply hold the pendulum in dowsing mode, give it a little movement and say your query aloud. It's said that the pendulum will swing in a circle for yes and back and forth for no. Remember, there is no proof that this works at all and, particularly in the case of small children, it's best to keep your questions fun!

## FUN FACT

Dowsing has been practised for thousands of years, but has never been proved scientifically to work. Some believe that it uses magnetic fields, others that dowsers tune into the 'energy' of water, treasure, long-buried buildings. But many others, including most scientists, maintain that it's the dowser themselves that unconsciously (or consciously) move the pendulum.

# Templates

All the templates shown here will need enlarging. Simply scan them, double-check your settings and make sure they print to your preferred enlarged size, then cut them out.

**Paper Village**
Pages 44–45

To make the Paper Village, scan both of these pages, enlarge, print and cut out both templates before sticking them together with tape.

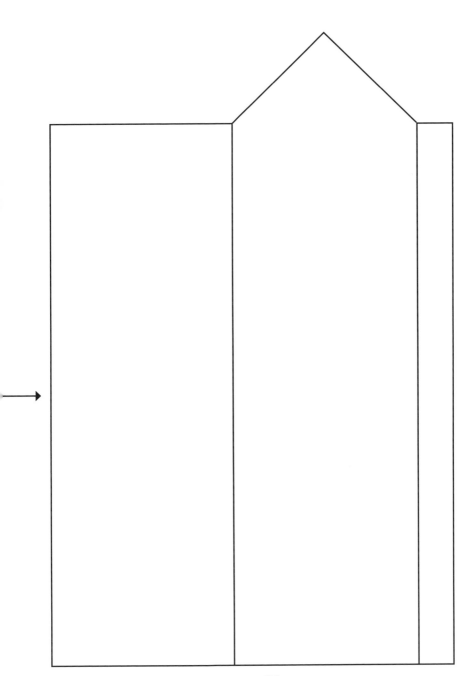

**Winged Headband**
Pages 20–21

**Blooming Flowers**
Pages 22–23

**Garland – Flagging It Up**
Page 106

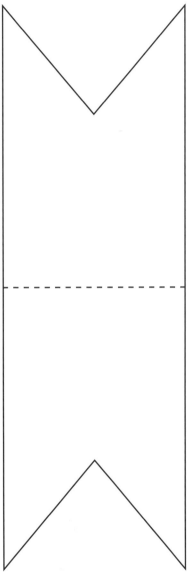

# Acknowledgements

Thanks to Loulou Cousin and Jeff Pitcher for their making skills and inspiration. The superstar kids: Arthur, Dusty, Jackson, Dee Dee, Arthur, Agnes, Edward and Emily. My agent, Juliet Pickering, and everyone at Blake Friedmann. Sarah, Stacey and Katherine at Quadrille for their enthusiasm and expertise. Penny for her cheerleading and incredible photography. Alice for her superior prop-choosing powers.

ABOUT
THE
AUTHOR

Kate Hodges has written seven books that have been translated into eight languages. Her titles include biography collections *Warriors, Witches, Women* and *I Know A Woman*. She has also written guides to London, among them *Little London*, *Rural London*, *Welcome to the Dark Side: Occult London* and *London in an Hour*, and family activity book *On a Starry Night*.

She has over 25 years' writing experience on magazines, having been a staffer on publications including *The Face*, *Bizarre*, *Just Seventeen* and *Sky*, and has written for many more. She currently writes regularly for *The Green Parent* and *Shindig!* magazines. She has twins and lives in Hastings. In her spare time, she plays in bands Ye Nuns and The Hare and Hoofe.

@theekatehodges
www.katehodges.org

**Publishing Director:** Sarah Lavelle
**Commissioning Editor:** Sarah Thickett
**Editor:** Stacey Cleworth
**Copy-editor:** Gillian Haslam
**Proofreader:** Catherine Jackson
**Art Direction and Design:** Katherine Keeble
**Photographer:** Penny Wincer
**Prop Stylist:** Alice King
**Head of Production:** Stephen Lang
**Senior Production Controller:** Katie Jarvis

Published in 2021 by Quadrille,
an imprint of Hardie Grant Publishing

Quadrille
52–54 Southwark Street
London SE1 1UN
quadrille.com

Cataloguing in Publication Data: a catalogue record for this
book is available from the British Library.

ISBN 978 1 78713 718 9

Printed in China